Aces 3

By W. Wayne Patton

Color by W. Wayne Patton and Don Greer

Illustrated by W. Wayne Patton

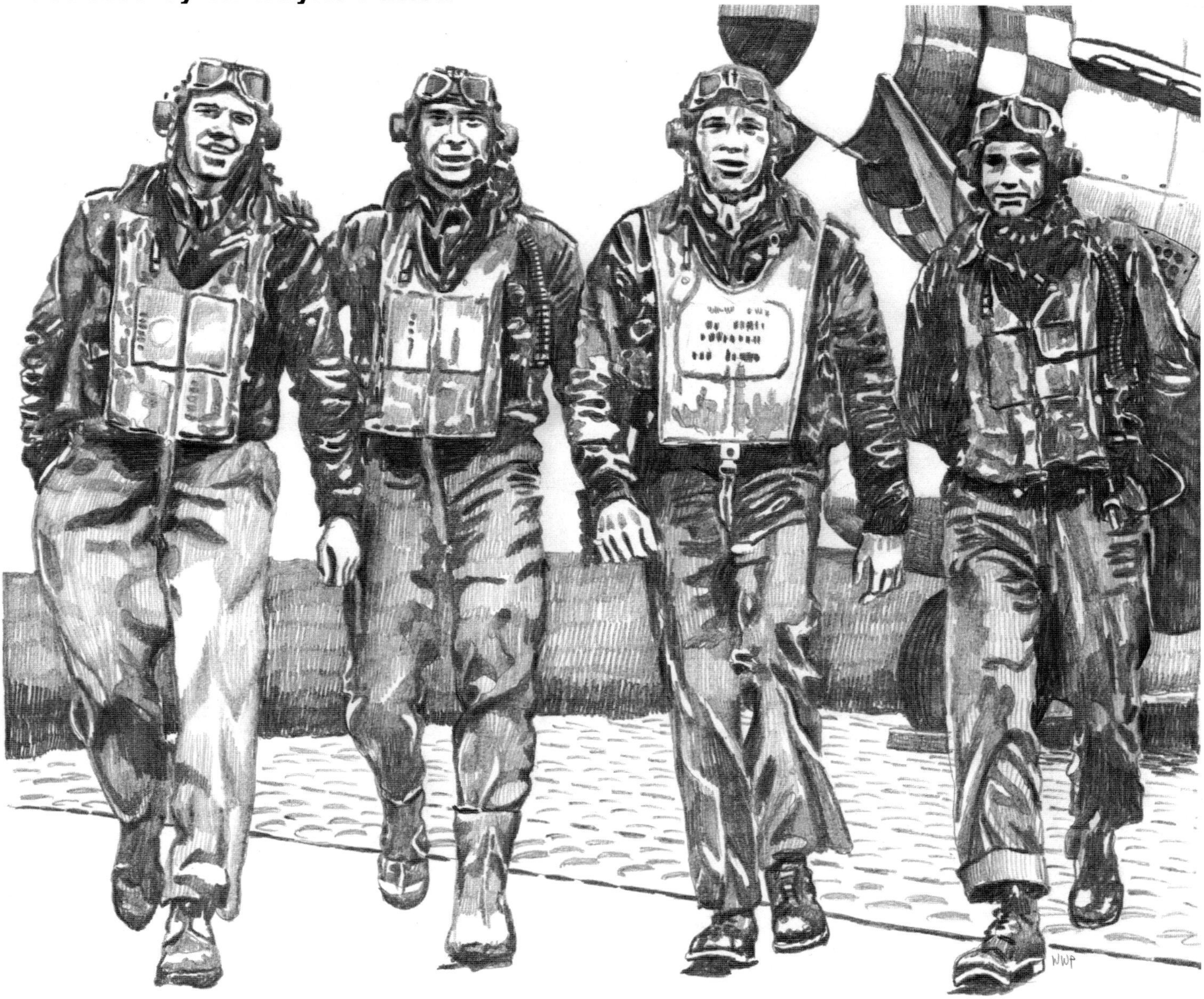

squadron/signal publications

Austrian ace Walter Nowotny, flying an Fw 190A, shoots down a Soviet LaGG-3 fighter over the thawing Russian steppes in the spring of 1943. The Russian pilot crashed in the snow to become Nowotny's 135th kill. Nowotny ultimately scored 258 aerial victories, the last few while flying the Me 262A jet fighter.

Acknowledgements

I would like to acknowledge the assistance of the following institutions, publications and individuals in the preparation of this book.

Institutions:

National Air and Space Museum (NASM), Washington DC
US National Archives, Washington DC
Imperial War Museum, London
RAF Museum, Hendon, London
US Air Force Museum, Dayton, Ohio

Publications:

"Air Aces," C. Shores, Presidio Press, 1983.
"Japanese Naval Aces and Fighter Units in WWII," I. Hata and Y. Izawa, Naval Institute Press, 1989.
"Medalled Pilots of the Japanese Army Air Force in WWII," Model Art Extra #416, 1993.
"Heroes of the Imperial Japanese Navy Air Force—1935-1945," Model Art Extra #439, 1994.
"Above the Lines," "Above the Trenches," and "Over the Lines," N. Franks, F. Bailey and R. Guest, Grub Street, 1992 and 1996.
Federal Standard Colors, 1994.
"Stalin's Eagles," H.D. Seidl, Schiffer, 1998.
"American Fighter Aces Album," Edited by Col. J. Ward Boyce, USAS Ret., 1996.
"Allied Fighter Aces of World War II," Mike Spick, Stackpole Books, 1997.
"Chinese MiG Ace Over Korea," Bob Bergin, in Military History Magazine, December 2001.
"MiG Alley," Larry Davis, Squadron/Signal Publications, 1978.
"P-51 Mustang Aces," William N. Hess, Motorbooks, 1992.
"Tiger Ace," Gary L. Simpson, Schiffer, 1994.
"Panzer Aces," Franz Kurowski, Fedorowics, 1992.
"Luftwaffe Fighter Aces," Mike Spick, Stackpole, 1996.
"Victory Roll!" William Wolf, Schiffer, 2001.

ISBN 0-89747-472-4

If you have any photographs of aircraft, armor, soldiers or ships of any nation, particularly wartime snapshots, why not share them with us and help make Squadron/Signal's books all the more interesting and complete in the future. Any photograph sent to us will be copied and the original returned. The donor will be fully credited for any photos used. Please send them to:

Squadron/Signal Publications, Inc.
1115 Crowley Drive
Carrollton, TX 75011-5010

Если у вас есть фотографии самолётов, вооружения, солдат или кораблей любой страны, особенно, снимки времён войны, поделитесь с нами и помогите сделать новые книги издательства Эскадрон/Сигнал ещё интереснее. Мы переснимем ваши фотографии и вернём оригиналы. Имена приславших снимки будут сопровождать все опубликованные фотографии. Пожалуйста, присылайте фотографии по адресу:

Squadron/Signal Publications, Inc.
1115 Crowley Drive
Carrollton, TX 75011-5010

軍用機、装甲車両、兵士、軍艦などの写真を所持しておられる方はいらっしゃいませんか？どの国のものでも結構です。作戦中に撮影されたものが特に良いのです。Squadron/Signal社の出版する刊行物において、このような写真は内容を一層充実し、興味深くすることができます。当方にお送り頂いた写真は、複写の後お返しいたします。出版物中に写真を使用した場合は、必ず提供者のお名前を明記させて頂きます。お写真は下記にご送付ください。

Squadron/Signal Publications, Inc.
1115 Crowley Drive
Carrollton, TX 75011-5010

Individuals:

David and Yumiko Luke
Matt and Yulia Crockett
Kevin Patton
Gary Simpson
Patrick Stein
Paul Terry

Dedication:

To my father, William J Patton.

Editor's Note:

FS numbers given are an approximate guide to actual colors.

(Title Page) Four leading aces of the 357th Fighter Group walk away from a P-51D Mustang. These men are (from left): Major Richard A. Peterson (15.5 victories), Major Leonard 'Kit' Carson (18.5), Major John B. England (17.5) and Major Clarence E. 'Bud' Anderson (16.25). Anderson's story is chronicled in this book.

(Back Cover) Han De-cai's MiG-15*bis* shoots down the F-86F of Capt Harold E. Fischer over Manchuria on 7 April 1953. This is Han's fifth victory and he went on to a long career with the Chinese People's Liberation Army Air Force. Fischer – a ten-victory ace with the 51st Fighter-Interceptor Wing – was unable to glide back to his base and bailed out over Manchuria. Chinese forces promptly captured him and held him at Mukden until his release in 1955. Fischer ultimately served a lengthy career with the USAF.

Aces

The Aces series talks about aces, their machines, and their tactics. Emphasis is placed on air aces, with occasional coverage of other aces, such as tank and submarine commanders, to provide contrast.

What is an ace? Air aces are fighter pilots with five or more aerial victories over enemy aircraft. Tank aces must destroy five or more enemy tanks, while submarine commanders must sink 50,000 tons of shipping or five ships to reach ace status. Targets must be seen by witnesses to catch fire, explode, be deserted by their crews, sink, or crash. Enemy machines must contain people to be counted as 'kills.' Barrage balloons and World War Two V1 'buzz bombs' did not count toward ace status because no people were on board those vehicles. Controversy continues to this day, because the North Vietnamese Peoples' Air Force (NVPAF) allowed its fighter pilots to claim victories over unmanned reconnaissance drones as 'kills.'

One of the first aces to be acclaimed as such was the World War One French fighter pilot Jean Navarre (12 kills). French newspapers of the period made a hero out of Navarre and started the 'ace' or 'top card' concept. Navarre had five kills to his credit at the time. That number, almost by chance, became the official mark at which point a fighter pilot could be designated an ace.

Confirmation of Kills

The Bukosho was Japan's equivalent of the British Victoria Cross or the American Medal of Honor

Photographs, gun camera film, or radar images can also be used to confirm victories. In the 1991 Gulf War and other recent conflicts, missile kills were made over the horizon and consequently could not be seen by the pilot. In these cases, radar can show an aircraft breaking up or crashing and was used to confirm 'kills.'

Different countries have used many processes for determining air ace status. Germany had the most precise and possibly the simplest definition. In both world wars, they had a strict 'one pilot, one victory' rule. One pilot was given a victory credit for each enemy aircraft shot down. If another pilot assisted him, the other pilot got no credit to his overall score for the 'assist.' Pilots sometimes flipped a coin to see who got the kill. Some top aces, like Walter Nowotny, gave kills to wingmen or new pilots to bolster their feeling of self-worth. German fighter pilots had to have at least one witness to their 'kills,' fill out comprehensive victory reports, and a combat report to claim a victory. German victory totals in World War Two are considered highly accurate and are usually on the low side. Germany considered pilots scoring ten or over victories to be *experten* (experts), while most other countries considered pilots scoring over five victories to be aces.

The French method of assigning kills during World War One was much like the simple method used by the Germans. During World War Two, the French introduced a complex system that allowed several fighter pilots participating in an aerial victory to claim whole 'kills.' French fighter pilots were also assigned a whole 'kill' for probable victories. This means French World War Two aces like Camille Plubeau (14) (See Aces, 6077, from Squadron/Signal Publications) would have scored far fewer kills if they had used fractions like the Americans or flipped a coin like the Germans. Several French aces that flew with the British and Soviets during World War Two have tried to use the French system to compute their scores. For this reason, Pierre Clostermann's score is listed as 33 'kills' (using the French system) and 19 'kills' (using the British system).

During World War Two, the *Regia Aeronautica* (Royal Italian Air Force) used the same method employed by the French. The Italians always assigned full 'kills' for shared and probable victories. This resulted in Italian fighter pilot scores being somewhat inflated, like those of the French.

Soviet fighter pilots have always reported their victories as 'personal kills' along with 'group or shared kills.' For example, the Soviet ace Grigori Rechkalov (see Aces 2, 6084, from Squadron/Signal Publications) finished World War Two with 56 personal kills, plus another five shared kills. They placed emphasis on the personal kills much like the Germans. The Soviets, Chinese, and North Koreans used the same system during the Korean War.

The Austrian ace Walter Nowotny was reported to have given victories to his wingmen.

Both the British Royal Air Force (RAF) and the United States Army Air Forces (USAAF; USAF from 1947) used fractions to calculate the group or shared kills. For example, the American ace Duane Beeson (See Aces 2) ended World War Two with a score of 17.33 kills. During World War One, the British used a complicated system of destroyed, forced down, and out of control designations to assign kills, while the Americans used the simple World War One French system. The British and Americans assigned kills made by night fighters or heavy day fighters during both world wars to only the pilot. The Americans reversed this during the Vietnamese War and assigned one kill to the pilot and one to his 'back-seater'[1] for each enemy aircraft shot down. America had only two ace pilots in the Vietnam War and three 'back-seaters' also made 'ace.' This author treats such teams as 'ace crews,' with the victory credit assigned only to the pilot. This is consistent with both tank and submarine kills. During the Arab-Israeli Wars, the Israeli Air Force used fractions to assign shared kills to fighter pilots – the same as the USAF and RAF.

No country had assigned destroyed, unmanned craft to fighter pilots as kills – at least until the NVPAF started this practice during the Vietnam War. The North Vietnamese used the French system of reporting and assigning kills and further confused the issue by counting destroyed Ryan Firebee reconnaissance drones as 'kills.' A close look at the scores of the 12 NVPAF 'aces' shows that perhaps three of them would be aces using the American system. Many of them took full credit for shared kills and several counted drones among their scores.

The Finnish Air Force verified and assigned kills based on the German system during World War Two. Similar to the Germans, certain Finnish pilots like Eino Luukkannen (56) (See Aces I) ran up large scores with fractional victories decided with a coin toss.

The author strongly feels that 'kills' should not be assigned for shooting down unmanned, reconnaissance drones used by the USAF over Vietnam. Likewise, a 'kill' should not be awarded twice, to the pilot and a 'back-seater,' but should be issued to the team with the pilot, tank commander, or captain keeping score. A heavy fighter operated by a crew is no different than a tank with a commander and crew. Several fighter pilots should not each be awarded a whole victory for a shared kill. The NVPAF violated two of these rules during the Vietnam War by calling fractional kills whole victories and by allowing destroyed reconnaissance drones to be assigned as kills.

Victory tallies should not be mistaken for points systems used by some air forces to assign awards or medals. For example, the destruction of a B-29 heavy bomber was worth far more to Japanese

[1]US Air Force 'back-seaters' were called Weapons System Officers (WSOs). US Navy and Marine 'back-seaters' were originally known as Radar Intercept Officers (RIOs), which were later renamed Naval Flight Officers (NFOs).

Jean Navarre was the first great French ace of World War One. Deflectors bolted to the propeller were an early attempt to allow machine gun bullets to pass through rotating propeller blades.

Grigori Rechkalov – wearing a chest full of medals – scored 56 personal and five shared victories during the Great Patriotic War.

pilots during the last days of World War Two than ten victories over fighters. Some fighter pilots were given the Bukosho, equivalent to the US Congressional Medal of Honor, for destroying one or two B-29s, but they were not aces. Another example is the points system used by the Luftwaffe to reward pilots for shooting down four engine bombers (four points) as opposed to fighters (one point). A fighter pilot gaining 40 or so points on the Western Front was awarded the Knight's Cross.

Air Forces and Fighter Pilots

Over time, approximately five percent of fighter pilots accounted for forty percent of the total claimed victories. The question has often been asked about which qualities set these high scoring pilots apart from the other pilots. During wartime, all air forces wish they had more aces. Since there have always been more young men and women wanting to be fighter pilots during peace time than there were actual positions for them, bean counters have created ways to weed them out that also may eliminate future aces. For example, some World War One aces – such as the 20-kill German ace Otto Kissenberth – wore eyeglasses. Until recently in the USAF and USN, no nation – except for Russia – has allowed women to become fighter pilots. Some Soviet women, particularly Lilya Litviak (12 kills), became aces. The discrimination of women has probably taken many future aces out of action before they had a chance to prove themselves. Many American pilots just before and during World War Two were 'washed out' of fighter pilot training because of poor marksmanship. Several slow starting German fighter pilots, like Gerhard Barkhorn (301), went on to become top aces. Some nations tried to get rid of aces not fitting the 'military mold.' For example, Sada-aki Akamatsu (37+) was broken in rank several times for insubordination, being drunk, or starting fights. The great Malta ace George 'Screwball' Beurling (31) was actually kicked out of the Royal Canadian Air Force for insubordination at a time when they needed good pilots. It seems that the modern Israeli Air Force may have part of the answer. They recruit fighter pilots like Ashir Snir (13.5) in high school, where they choose young men who are aggressive in sports and are good enough students able to learn modern flight systems. They put these youngsters into pilot training and – by age 18 – some of them are flying the most modern fighter jets Israel can lay its hands on. In the United States, the Air Force recruits from college graduates, already 22 years old and then by the time they go through another two years of training, they are the ripe old age of 24 or 25 years old. Gregory 'Pappy' Boyington was 26 years old when his 20-year-old squadron mates gave him his nickname during World War Two.

Twenty-kill ace Otto Kissenberth wore eyeglasses during World War One combat.

Lilya Litviak scored 12 kills over Stalingrad to become the world's highest scoring female ace. The Soviet regime was the only government to allow female fighter pilots to enter combat during the Great Patriotic War.

The Readers Talk

Several readers have taken the time to write to me about the subject matter in my books and for that I am grateful. Such comments make any publication better. For example, I received a letter from Mr. Patrick Stein, who had spoken with Adolph Galland in 1960 when the general was working a Heinkel/Potez booth at the Paris Air Show (please see page 59 in Aces 2). According to Mr. Stein, Galland indicated that since maintenance and aircraft availability was an unsure thing, he flew a number of Me 262s while with JV 44. He thought that one of his jets was marked with the 'Mickey Mouse' insignia in a similar manner as his old Bf 109F when flying with JG 26. Such a color scheme has shown up in several publications, including the IPMS Quarterly. Mr. Stein goes on to say that during discussions with many people, including former members of JV 44, no one could recall seeing an Me 262 marked like the one Galland had described to him. Thus, says Mr. Stein, the jet with the 'Mickey Mouse' marking probably did not exist.

Mr. Paul Terry from England wrote another highly interesting letter regarding a note sent to him by Spitfire ace George Unwin. In his note, Mr. Unwin emphatically states that he was not shot down on 5 November 1940 by Bf 109s (see pages 47 and 48 in Aces). The only time he was ever shot down was by a Dornier Do 17 rear gunner on 11 September 1940. This is great information that caused this author to dig deeper into his German sources. These and British sources show that Flight Sergeant George 'Grumpy' Unwin of No 19 Squadron did engage Bf 109E fighters of 9./JG 26 over the English Channel on 5 November 1940. Unwin's lone Spitfire (P7427) was so badly shot up that *Hauptmann* Gerhard Schopfel submitted a claim for this and one other Spitfire shot down that day. He received confirmation and both Spitfires were part of his final tally of 40 victories. Obviously, since Unwin was not shot down as Schopfel claimed, the latter should not have received confirmation for a kill. German sources say the Spitfire dove down through the clouds out of control. This author should have checked British records from that day, which clearly state that Unwin and his Spitfire made it back to his base. Unwin and Schopfel did clash in those channel skies long ago, but the outcome was different than the German version (please see Spitfire Mark I/II Aces 1939-41, Osprey Aircraft of the Aces number 12, page 77 for more information). Thank you Mr. Terry and Mr. Unwin for your letter and attached note.

Japanese naval ace Sada-aki Akamatsu (37+ kills) was brilliant in the air, but tended to be a hell-raiser. He was broken in rank several times during his career.

Ashir Snir flew both Mirages and F-4s for the Israeli Air Force. He ended his operational career with 13.5 kills.

The Korean War and the MiG-15

Some highly interesting information is slowly becoming available about the Korean War, now that the 'Iron Curtain' is an artifact of the past. Much of the information we were given during and after the Korean War has been 'one-sided' and much of it verging on propaganda. For example, it is now known that Soviet pilots – including many top World War Two aces – flew Mikoyan-Gurevich MiG-15 fighters with North Korean markings from bases near Andun, Manchuria at the time. At least two of these Soviet pilots, Nikolaj Vsilyevich Sutyagin (22) and Yevgenij Georgiyevich Pepelyaev (19), scored more kills than Joseph McConnell (16), America's top scorer. Additionally, the often-seen kill-to-loss ratio of ten MiG-15s shot down to one Sabre destroyed is propaganda. The Soviets say that four MiG-15s shot down for one Sabre destroyed is the true ratio. Allied fighter pilots got the worst of it when straight wing jets like Meteors, F-80 Shooting Stars, F-84 Thunderjets, and F9F Panthers are added into the mix. The Soviet pilots in their superior MiG-15*bis* fighter jets gave out much more against these inferior jets than they received. The kill ratio might be closer to three-to-one or even two-to-one with the straight wing jets considered; however, when the Chinese and North Korean MiG pilots are added, the kill ratio favors the American pilots. This author thinks after careful study that the kill ratio is approximately four-to-one in favor of the Allied pilots.

A myth was also built up around the MiG-15 that led US pilots to think the jet was better than it was. American officials offered a large cash reward for the first MiG-15 delivered to them. North Korean Peoples' Air Force pilot Ro Kim Suk flew his MiG-15*bis* to Kimpo Air Base days after the war ended and received $100,000 (nearly one million in today's dollars) for his Soviet-built jet. Major Chuck Yeager and Captain Tom Collins, two of the best test pilots of the time, thoroughly tested this fighter in Taiwan. This testing started to tell the real truth about Soviet fighters of the time. The MiG-15*bis* climbed better and reached higher altitudes than the F-86F, which was marginally faster and could dive far better because it was heavier than the MiG. F-86 pilots had to maneuver in the horizontal plane because a climbing turn could allow the better climbing MiGs an advantage. The MiG could not dive with a Sabre because of wing structure and design problems. The MiG was also greatly affected by compressibility forces, which caused control surfaces to freeze up in a dive.

The first MiG-15 fighters sent to Korea had pneumatic control systems that relied on air pressure rather than oil pressure to activate the flaps and rudder. Leaks often plagued these fighters and the MiG-15*bis* deployed to Korea had hydraulic systems that used oil pressure to activate the control surfaces. Early MiGs were left in a natural metal finish like most USAF Sabres, which was said to add to the top speed of both fighters. High-speed jet combat showed that the MiG-15*bis* fighters were not quite as good as the Allies thought they were. Soviet combat pilots put the following list together which was sent to officials at the MiG design bureau:

1. The air brakes needed to be larger to slow the sleek MiG-15 down more quickly. Late MiG-15*bis* fighters were equipped with larger 'Korean Model' air brakes.
2. More fuel was needed to increase flight time. Late MiG-15*bis* fighters were equipped with under wing drop tanks, similar to those carried by the Sabres.
3. Combat pilots wanted roomier cockpits with better rearward vision, although MiG-15s were equipped with bubble-type canopies. This was not changed on the MiG-15*bis*, but new models of the MiG-17 had taller and somewhat roomier cockpits.
4. Combat pilots wanted more speed (past Mach 0.92) in a dive, because Sabres could out-dive them to speeds of Mach 0.98 and beyond. There was no easy solution, since the heavier Sabres continued to outdive MiG-15s over Korea.
5. The aluminum wing skin needed to be thicker and riveted down better, because the skin pulled up at speeds near Mach 0.92 and altered the wing's aerodynamics. This one proved impossible to correct in the MiG-15 due to the way the wings were manufactured, but was later corrected on the MiG-17.
6. Pilots wanted a functioning artificial horizon. This was fixed on later MiG-15*bis* fighters.
7. Combat pilots requested an improved radio and homing beacon to locate downed aircraft. It is unknown whether or not these changes were made.
8. Combat pilots wanted improved handling at high altitude and high speed. They had to wait until the MiG-17 for these corrections.
9. A better cockpit heater was needed. No wonder Soviet pilots had a hard time fitting into the small MiG-15 cockpits—they were covered in bulky clothing!
10. Combat pilots wanted an effective gravity resistance suit (g-suit),which Sabre pilots already had. They received a crude version before the end of the Korean War.
11. Combat pilots wanted an improvement in cockpit armor for better pilot protection. The MiG-15 was not upgraded, but the MiG-17 and later MiG-19 did receive better armor protection.
12. Combat pilots wanted camouflaged paint jobs on the MiGs rather than shiny natural metal, which Sabre pilots could see at great distances. It has long been said that no camouflaged MiG-15s were seen over Korea; however, good Soviet sources firmly state that camouflaged MiG-15*bis* 'Korean' models did reach units at Andun before the Korean War ended. Refer to the illustration on page 7 of Fedoret's MiG-15*bis* 'Korean Model' with the larger air brake and three color paint scheme.

Major Frederick C. Blesse

Frederick 'Boots' Blesse grew up in the military as the son of a career Army physician. He was born in the Panama Canal Zone on 22 August 1921. Blesse entered the US Military Academy at West Point, New York in 1941 and received his wings and commission on 5 June 1945.

Blesse was assigned to the 1st Fighter Squadron (FS), 413th Fighter Group (FG) at Okinawa, but World War Two was nearly over and Blesse scored no kills. Returning to the United States, he was assigned to the 56th FG at Selfridge Field, Michigan flying the new F-80 Shooting Star jet fighter. Blesse volunteered for combat duty after the Korean War began in June of 1950. On 11 November 1950, he flew his first ground support combat mission in an F-51 (formerly P-51) Mustang. After 67 missions, he was transferred to the 49th Fighter Bomber Group (FBG) and flew another 121 missions in the straight-wing F-80 Shooting Star. This jet was outdated by the swept-wing Soviet-built MiG-15 in the Korean skies.

Blesse transferred to the 94th Fighter-Interceptor Squadron (FIS), 1st Fighter-Interceptor Group (FIG), flying F-86 Sabres at George Air Force Base (AFB), California. He volunteered for a second combat tour after eight months at George. Blesse was stationed at Kimpo Air Base (AB), Korea in March of 1952 flying F-86E-10-NA Sabres with the 334th FIS. He scored his first victory over a MiG-15 during his first engagement on 25 May 1952. The aggressive Blesse quickly claimed eight more MiG-15s and a piston-engine Lavochkin La-9 to become a double ace. His gunnery excellence was later demonstrated during the 1955 Air Force Gunnery Meet, when he won all six individual performance trophies while flying an F-86F Sabre. He always turned into attacks and favored hit-and-run attacks where he could fire and keep going in the heavier F-86. MiG aces, on the other hand, usually climbed away from the fight in their fast climbing fighters. Blesse did not like the Sabre's .50 caliber (12.7MM) machine guns and recommended their replacement by cannon. He got missiles instead, and flew 108 missions with the 366th Tactical Fighter Wing (TFW) over North Vietnam,where he scored no further victories. Blesse served a second tour in Vietnam as Seventh Air Force Assistant Director of Operations and retired as a major general in April of 1975.

Kapitan (Captain) Nikolaj Vasilyevich Sutyagin

Sutyagin was born in the Gorkij area on 5 May 1923 and entered military service in 1941. He qualified as a pilot the following year and entered combat against the Japanese in 1945, but scored no victories during the Great Patriotic War.

Sutyagin made up for lost time while flying the MiG-15*bis* over Korea. Assigned to the 17 IAP (*Istrebitel'nyy Aviatsionnyy Polk*—Fighter Aviation Regiment), he scored his first kill over North Korea on 19 June 1951. Sutyagin quickly claimed three more kills over the next three days, shot down an Australian Gloster Meteor a few days later, then downed another Meteor on 26 September 1951. He was awarded the Gold Star of Hero of the Soviet Union on 10 October 1951. Sutyagin claimed five more Allied jets over the Yalu River during December. In January of 1952, he added three more jets to his most respectable tally of 22 personal victories. He shot down 15 F-86 Sabres, two F-80 Shooting Stars, three F-84 Thunderjets, and two Meteors for his total of 22 kills. Sutyagin ended the Korean War as a *Kapitan* (Captain), deputy squadron leader, and the world's number one jet ace of all time.

Sutyagin remained in the VVS (*Voyenno-Vozdushniye Sily*; Military Air Forces) after rotating out of combat in February of 1952. He graduated from the Air Force Academy in 1964, retired as a General Major in 1978, and passed away on 12 November 1986.

Polkovnik (Colonel) Yevgenij Georgiyevich Pepelyaev

Pepelyaev was born in the Irkutsk area on 18 March 1918 and started his military career in 1936. He won his wings two years later and was posted to the 300 IAP (*Istrebitel'nyy Aviatsionnyy Polk*—Fighter Aviation Regiment) in the Soviet Far East.

He became a squadron leader there, but did not enter combat until November of 1943. Pepelyaev then flew the Yakovlev Yak-7B with the 162 IAP on the Byelorussian Front, where he encountered German aircraft several times without scoring. Pepelyaev was then transferred back to the 300 IAP in the Far East, where he took part in final operations against the Japanese. Although he was occupied with ground support duties, he managed to fly 30 missions on Yak-9Ts and destroyed one locomotive. He again scored no aerial victories over the Japanese. He was promoted to command the regiment at Mukden.

In late 1947, Pepelyaev was assigned as deputy commander of the 196 IAP and was simultaneously promoted to *Podpolkovnik* (Lieutenant Colonel). He went with his unit to China – where they were working up on the new MiG-15s – as its commander during January of 1951. He then moved to Antung, Manchuria, near the North Korean border. Pepelyaev's superior was Ivan Kozhedub (62 kills in World War Two), Commander of the 324 IAD (*Istrebietel Aviatsionnaya Divislya*—Fighter Aviation Division). The 196 IAP claimed

***Polkovnik* (Colonel) Yevgenij Pepelyaev was a MiG-15*bis* ace and a formidable leader during the Korean War.**

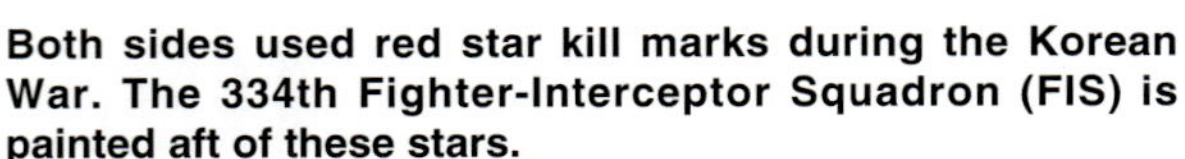

Both sides used red star kill marks during the Korean War. The 334th Fighter-Interceptor Squadron (FIS) is painted aft of these stars.

Major Frederick C. 'Boots' Blesse of the 334th FIS flew this North American F-86E-10-NA Sabre (51-2821). The Sabre was overall natural metal, with Orange-Yellow (FS33538) and Black theater bands around the fuselage and wings. Blesse used red stars as kill marks below his cockpit. The Squadron insignia was also painted under the cockpit. This Sabre is now displayed at the Champlin Fighter Museum in Mesa, Arizona.

Kapitan **(Captain) Nikolaj Sutyagin flew this Mikoyan-Gurevich MiG-15*****bis*** **(Red 132) of the 17 IAP (*****Istrebitel'nyy Aviatsionnyy Polk*****; Fighter Aviation Regiment), 303 IAD (*****Istrebitel'nyy Aviatsionnaya Divisiya*****; Fighter Aviation Division). This Division was attached to the North Korean Air Force from June of 1951 to February of 1952. Sutyagin claimed all his 22 kills while flying this fighter. The MiG-15*****bis*** **was overall natural metal, with a red (FS21350) nose band and upper tail.**

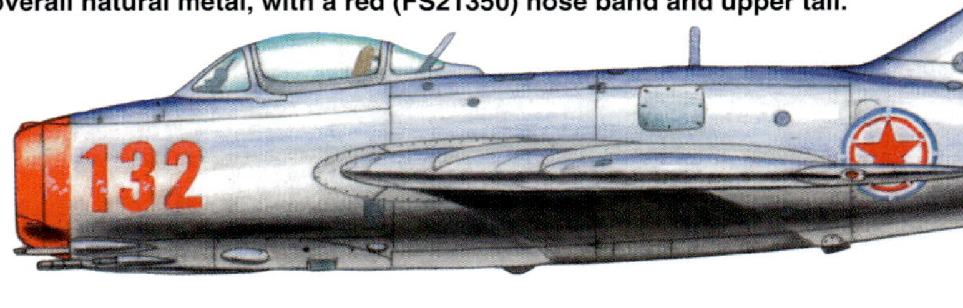

This North Korean Air Force MiG-15***bis*** **(Red 325) was flown by** ***Polkovnik*** **(Colonel) Yevgenij Pepelyaev of the 196 IAP, 303 IAD from June of 1951 to January of 1952. This fighter was overall natural metal, with a red (FS21350) nose and North Korean national markings. This jet had been damaged in combat and repainted in these markings (see Aces 1).**

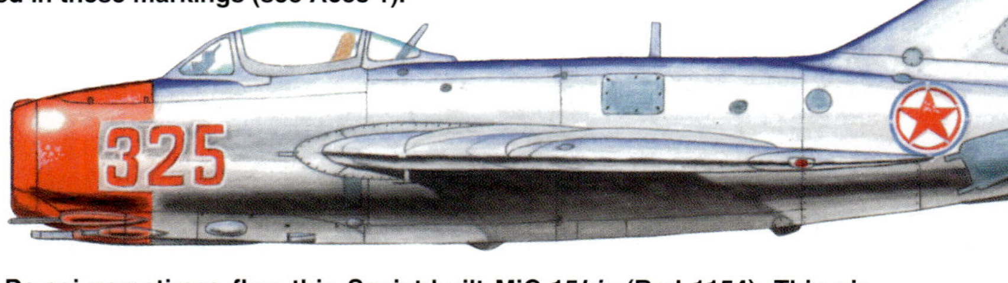

Rankless Chinese ace Han De-cai sometimes flew this Soviet-built MiG-15***bis*** **(Red 1154). This aircraft is similar to the one (Red 1152) in which he shot down USAF Captain Harold E. Fischer on 7 April 1953. Markings on the jet are similar to those above. Both sides used red star kill marks.**

Captain Harold E. Fischer flew the PAPER TIGER, an F-86F-10-NA Sabre (51-12958) when he was with the 39th FIS, 51st Fighter-Interceptor Wing (FIW). He was probably shot down in this fighter by Chinese ace Han De-cai. Fischer bailed out, but was captured and held by the Chinese at Mukden until released in May of 1955.

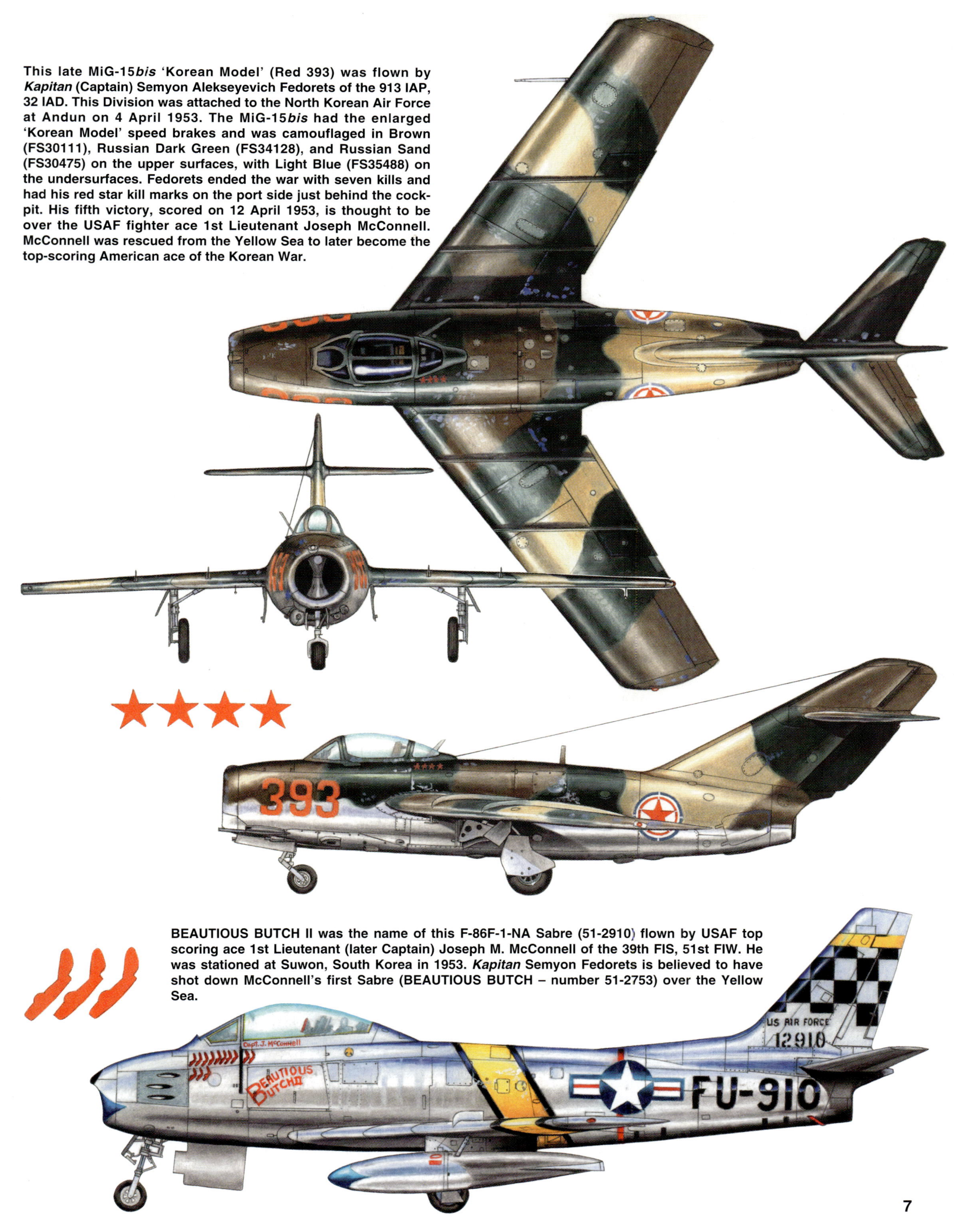

This late MiG-15*bis* 'Korean Model' (Red 393) was flown by *Kapitan* (Captain) Semyon Alekseyevich Fedorets of the 913 IAP, 32 IAD. This Division was attached to the North Korean Air Force at Andun on 4 April 1953. The MiG-15*bis* had the enlarged 'Korean Model' speed brakes and was camouflaged in Brown (FS30111), Russian Dark Green (FS34128), and Russian Sand (FS30475) on the upper surfaces, with Light Blue (FS35488) on the undersurfaces. Fedorets ended the war with seven kills and had his red star kill marks on the port side just behind the cockpit. His fifth victory, scored on 12 April 1953, is thought to be over the USAF fighter ace 1st Lieutenant Joseph McConnell. McConnell was rescued from the Yellow Sea to later become the top-scoring American ace of the Korean War.

BEAUTIOUS BUTCH II was the name of this F-86F-1-NA Sabre (51-2910) flown by USAF top scoring ace 1st Lieutenant (later Captain) Joseph M. McConnell of the 39th FIS, 51st FIW. He was stationed at Suwon, South Korea in 1953. *Kapitan* Semyon Fedorets is believed to have shot down McConnell's first Sabre (BEAUTIOUS BUTCH – number 51-2753) over the Yellow Sea.

F-86 Sabres during their first dogfight on 2 April. Pepelyaev notched up his first kill during May, when he dived onto an unsuspecting F-86 and steadily fired into the Sabre while it spun into the ground. After his first kill, he downed several Sabres by stalking them from above and hitting them when they least expected to be attacked. Pepelyaev was promoted to *Polkovnik* (Colonel) during August of 1951. He is said to have led his pilots in a surprise attack on 12 Lockheed F-94 Starfire fighters. Pepelyaev claimed one of the seven aircraft downed. These 'F-94s' were probably Republic F-84 Thunderjets, straight-wing jets that looked similar to the F-94. Some F-94s were used in Korea as night and all-weather fighters, but many more F-84 Thunderjets were employed as ground attack fighter-bombers in that conflict.

Pepelyaev shot down an F-86 on 15 July 1952, which brought his total to 19 personal kills. He was the second highest scoring jet ace of all time when he was ordered back to the Soviet Union. His 19 victories included 14 F-86 Sabres, two F-84 Thunderjets, two F-94s? (probably F-84s), and one F-80 Shooting Star. Some publications list his final score as 23 kills, but Soviet sources indicate that this figure included shared victories. Pepelyaev seems to have been a careful fighter pilot who preferred to stalk the enemy until just the right opportunity presented itself. He then attacked, usually from above and with the sun to his back. The attacks he led against straight-wing jets ended disasterously for the enemy. Pepelyaev was an expert shot and usually fired few shells in scoring his victories. He was a highly experienced and dangerous MiG-15*bis* pilot in the skies over Korea. He was a worthy foe of American F-86 Sabre pilots and he shot down a number of them.

Pepelyaev graduated from the General Staff Academy in 1958 and retired from active service in 1973.

Rankless (later *Zhong Jiang*–Lt. General) Han De-cai

Han De-cai was born to a peasant family in China's Anhui Province in 1933. He joined the People's Liberation Army (PLA) as a 16-year-old in 1949. During 1950, Chairman Mao Zedong asked for volunteers from the PLA to become pilots in a new air force to defend China. Han was one of these volunteers, and became a successful MiG-15 pilot and ace.

Han De-cai had little education and was posted to the Air Force Preparatory School. When the Korean War started in 1950, the 17-year-old Han was sent to the Air Academy to start pilot training. Like many pilots, he found that it was much harder to learn the theory of flight than to actually learn to fly. He and his fellow pilots had only three months to learn to fly. They spent 15 hours on the Yak-18 and another 15 hours on the Yak-11. Once with a combat unit, the Soviet instructors used the Yak-17 – a straight-wing jet similar to the F-80 Shooting Star – to train the new Chinese jet pilots. After only a few hours on Yak-17s, Han and his fellow pilots went to an advanced airfield where they first flew the new MiG-15. He was sent into combat with only 60 hours of flight time – including 30 hours on jets – against the better-trained Americans.

Soviet pilots taught only flight basics to the Chinese students, who had to work out tactics by themselves. The Air Force of the PLA (AFPLA) initially did not enter into combat with American formations and only later did they fight the Americans when they had superior numbers. Han and 11 other pilots engaged 12 F-80 Shooting Stars that were attacking a bridge over the Chinsan River on 24 March 1952. The American pilots had started their bombing runs when the 12 MiG-15s attacked, but quickly dropped their bombs and headed out to sea where they thought they would be safe. Han and others followed this time and he claimed two F-80s that he said fell into the sea. He had fired ahead of the F-80s to herd them back into a position where his gunnery was more effective. His fighter's horizontal stabilizer was damaged. Allied records show no fighter bombers lost on that day, but these records were incomplete in some cases .

Han De-cai was a five-kill Chinese MiG-15 ace by the end of the Korean War.

Following his engagement with theF-80s, Han went back to the Chinese interior to train on the new MiG-15*bis*, which had hydraulic controls instead of the MiG-15's pneumatic systems. He shot down a Sabre in a new MiG-15*bis* on 26 January 1953. The American pilot turned to the right at the same time Han and his element leader were also turning right. The F-86 passed between the two MiGs and Han who was flying wingman hit him with a quick deflection shot. Lt. Bill Stauffer of the 336th FIS/4th FIG piloted the F-86. Han shot down another F-86 on 26 March. That Sabre was part of a two-fighter decoy to lead the Chinese MiGs into a trap. When the two F-86s broke, the second one made a climbing turn which allowed Han in his faster climbing MiG to catch him and shoot him down. There is no record of a Sabre lost on this day.

Many Soviet and Chinese MiGs were clashing with US aircraft on 7 April 1953. An American F-86 pilot latched onto a Soviet-flown fighter, but when he saw another MiG – this time a Chinese-flown one – right in front of him, he quickly lined up on the fighter and fired scoring hits. Han's MiG was behind the F-86, which made violent maneuvers to escape. The American pilot, Captain Harold E. Fischer (ten kills), climbed to avoid mountains and Han was there waiting for him. He hit Fischer's jet and the latter bailed out over Manchuria, where he was taken prisoner.

After the Korean War ended, Han De-cai flew MiG-19 fighters, which he claimed were more difficult to fly than the MiG-15*bis*. He served in the prestigious position of vice commander of the Nanjing area and retired from the AFPLA with the rank of Lt. General. The PLA has had trouble deciding if it wants military ranks like other air forces. There were none at first, but ranks slowly began creeping into the Chinese AFPLA after 1985. Han De-cai now writes calligraphy and displays his work alongside his wife's paintings.

Captain Harold E. Fischer

Ohio native Harold Fischer attended both Iowa and Oklahoma State Universities. He was in Reserve Officer's Training Corps (ROTC) and was commissioned a Second Lieutenant in the Army before transferring to the USAF for flight training. He received his wings in 1951.

Fischer completed 150 missions flying F-80 Shooting Stars for the 80th Fighter-Bomber Squadron (FBS), 8th Fighter-Bomber Wing (FBW) in Korea. He then signed up for another tour in September of 1952 and was assigned to 39th Fighter-Interceptor Squadron (FIS), 51st Fighter-Interceptor Wing (FIW), which flew F-86 Sabres from Suwon AB, Korea.

Captain Harold E. Fischer shot down ten MiG-15s over Korea while flying F-86F Sabres.

The aggressive Fischer scored his first kill on 26 November 1952, after chasing a MiG across the Yalu River into Manchuria, which Allied pilots were not supposed to do. His second kill came on 22 December, after scaring a MiG pilot so badly that he ejected before Fischer had fired a shot. Kill number three came six days later for this aggressive fighter pilot. Fischer liked to fly into China after his victims and on 23 February 1953 he followed one all the way to its base near the Yalu River, where he shot it down while in its landing approach. The following day, he was vectored by ground radar to a flight of four MiGs near Chongchon and he chased one well into China before putting tracer rounds up its tailpipe, setting it on fire. He went on to destroy four more MiGs during February and was promoted to Captain. His tenth MiG fell to his guns in March of 1953.

Fischer was shot down either by Soviet ace Dmytry Yermakov (25 kills during World War Two) or by Chinese ace Han De-cai (five) on 7 April 1953. This occurred during a wild dogfight where Fischer shot up Han's flight leader. Both Fischer and this author believe that Han probably hit Fischer's engine, causing him to bail out over Chinese airspace. The Chinese held Fischer as a prisoner at Mukden until 31 May 1955.

Following the Korean War, Harold Fischer served in intelligence and later advised the South Vietnamese Air Force during the Vietnam War. He was a Colonel when he retired in May of 1978.

Kapitan (Captain) Semyon Alekseyevich Fedorets

Fedorets graduated from pilot training at the Odessa military flying school in 1944. He was then posted to the 403 IAP-PVO (*Istrebitel'nyy Aviatsionnyy Polk*–Fighter Aviation Regiment, *Protivovozdushnaya Oborona*–Soviet Air Defense Forces) on the Leningrad Front in 1944, which flew Lend-Lease Bell P-39 Airacobras. Fedorets did not have a chance to close with enemy aircraft during the Great Patriotic War – the Russian name for World War Two. He was posted to the 26 GIAP (*Gvardejskaya IAP*–Guards

Semyon Alekseyevich Fedorets was a Soviet pilot who flew MiG-15*bis* 'Korean Specials' during the Korean War. He shot down seven F-86 Sabres.

Fighter Aviation Regiment) in 1946, but was reassigned to the 913 IAP at Voskresenka in the Far East that September. The Regiment reported to the 64 IAK (*Istrebitel'nyy Aviatsionnyy Korpus*; Fighter Aviation Corps) in China in April of 1952. Fedorets was a flight leader when the unit was rotated to Andun, China, where most Soviet units were stationed during the Korean War.

Fedorets was an aggressive MiG pilot, who claimed an F-86 Sabre for his first victory on 17 December 1952. He had claimed another two Sabres by 21 February 1953. Fedorets shot down another Sabre on 3 March and he forced down the USAF fighter ace Captain Joseph McConnell in a running battle out over the Yellow Sea on 12 April. McConnell managed to bail out of his F-86E Beautious Butch into the Yellow Sea and was rescued by a US Navy helicopter. Fedorets' MiG was damaged by another F-86 during this same engagement and he was forced to bail out over land. His claim for McConnell was never confirmed because gun camera film was lost with his MiG. After Fedorets returned to his base at Andun, he shot down two additional Sabres. The seventh and last kill over Dapu airfield made him the 32 IAD's highest scoring ace. Fedorets seemed to like using flock shoot tactics, where the shock of his attack scattered enemy fighters and then he would pick off stragglers. He ended the Korean War with seven personal victories.

Captain Joseph M. McConnell

The highest scoring American fighter ace during the Korean War was actually 'washed out' of (failed) fighter pilot training during World War Two. Joseph M. McConnell went on to score 16 confirmed kills over Korea.

McConnell hailed from New Hampshire and joined the US Army in 1940. He was originally assigned to the Medical Corps before applying for and being accepted for flight training in 1943. He 'washed out' as a student pilot, but became a navigator and flew some 60 missions in B-24 Liberator heavy bombers over Germany.

In 1946, McConnell reapplied for pilot training and he evidently had it figured out this time as he was awarded his pilot's wings on 25 February 1948—just in time for the Korean War. McConnell was deployed to Korea in September of 1952 and flew with the 39th Fighter-Interceptor Squadron (FIS), 51st Fighter-Interceptor Wing (FIW). He claimed his first victory – a MiG-15 – on 14 January 1953, after which his score increased rapidly. By 16 February, he had shot down five MiGs to become an ace. McConnell had just recorded his eighth kill when Soviet MiG pilot Semyon Alekseyevich Fedorets (seven kills) hit his Sabre on 12 April 1953. McConnell was forced to bail out over the Yellow Sea, where a Navy helicopter quickly rescued him.

Joseph McConnell was America's top ace of the Korean War, with 16 victories.

McConnell had ten victories to his credit by the end of April, but his big week came in May. He destroyed six more MiGs between 13 and 18 May to close his combat career over Korea with 16 kills. He shot down three MiGs in one enggagment on 18 May while flying his last Korean Sabre, Beautious Butch II, which had red MiG kill marks painted on the nose.

Following the Korean War, McConnell became a test pilot at Edwards AFB, California. He was killed when a new F-86H Sabre he was flying crashed near Rogers Dry Lake bed on 25 August 1954.

McConnell was a highly aggressive fighter pilot with an 'I'll show you' attitude stemming from his 'washing out' of fighter pilot training during World War Two. He seemed to be in the middle of the fight much of his career in Korea. McConnell was an expert shot and liked diving down through MiG-15 formations with his guns blazing.

Chusa (Major) Yohei Hinoki

Yohei Hinoki of the Japanese Army Air Force's 64th *Sentai* (Army Air Group) is famous for his exploits over Burma, Singapore, and Southern China. He fought from the beginning of World War Two in early Nakajima Ki-43-1 *Hayabusa* (Peregrine Falcon – code name Oscar) fighters to the end of the war flying the lethal Kawasaki Ki-100-1-*Otsu*. He lost a leg to USAAF P-51s over China, but through superhuman effort he downed Mustangs over Japan in 1945.

Hinoki was born in 1919 and received his flight commission in June of 1941. He was then assigned to the 64th *Sentai*, the unit in which he achieved fame. He served in the Malayan campaign and was coached in the fine art of dog-fighting by the Nomonhan ace, *Shosa* (Captain) Iwori Sakai (15). (The Nomonhan Incident was fought between Japan and the Soviet Union along the Manchurian Border in 1939. Large air battles produced aces on both sides of the conflict. The Japanese won in the air, but Soviet ground forces flanked the Japanese and forced their withdrawal.)

Hinoki's skill with a Ki-43-1 led to his assignment as wingman to *Sentai* commander *Chusa* Tateo Kato, which initially limited his opportunities to engage enemy aircraft. Despite his wingman status, he shot down two No 238 Squadron Hawker Hurricane IIs over Singapore on 31 January 1942. The Ki-43-1 was lighter and more maneuverable than the Hurricane II.

On 10 April 1942, Hinoki fought a furious low-level dogfight against American Volunteer Group (AVG) ace Flight Leader Robert T. Smith (eight) over Loiwing, China. The Japanese pilot was severely wounded in the left arm and leg and his *Hayabusa* was shot up so badly that Smith – who confirmed another 'Oscar' kill that same day – claimed it as a probable after returning to his base. After escaping his attacker, Hinoki flew in great pain for two hours back to his base in Thailand, where he ran out of fuel during landing. Following a successful dead-stick landing, his parachute harness was found to have stopped a .50 caliber (12.7MM) round which would have cut short the *Hayabusa* ace's career. Hinoki spent a month recovering in the base hospital after this hair-raising encounter. He became the first Japanese pilot to shoot down an early P-51 fighter on 25 November 1943. Colonel Harry R. Melton Jr. of the 311th Fighter/Bomber Group bailed out of the P-51 and was captured by ground forces. Days later, Hinoki claimed another Mustang and a Lockheed P-38 Lightning that was escorting B-24 bombers of the 308th Bombardment Group (BG). He also shot down a 308th BG B-24 and damaged another — no mean feat in a lightly-armed fighter during one combat flight. While chasing other B-24s, Hinoki was attacked by another P-51 flown by 2Lt Robert F. Mulhollem (five). A .50 caliber bullet hit Hinoki in the right leg during this short fight. He barely managed to escape by diving and flying at treetop level away from Mulhollem, who claimed Hinoki's *Hayabusa* as a probable. Hinoki barely returned to his base, where his heavily wounded leg was amputated shortly after he landed. He spent months in the base hospital trying to build up enough strength to travel back to Japan.

Japanese Army Air Force hero and ace Yohei Hinoki stands in front of his Ki-43 *Hayabusa* fighter.

Once back in Japan, Hinoki became an instructor at the Akeno Fighter School because of his combat experience. He later flew combat missions equipped with an artificial leg – much like the RAF Spitfire ace Douglas Bader (26) – against B-29 Superfortress heavy bombers and their Mustang escort fighters.

On 16 July 1945, he led his Akeno headquarters flight against USAAF P-51D Mustangs of the 506th Fighter Group over Ise Bay. Hinoki and his pilots were flying the new and lethal Ki-100-1-*Otsu Goshikisen* (Type Three fighter), which was at least equal in performance to the Mustang. Hinoki closed to within 60 feet (18.3 M) of a Mustang flown by Capt. John W. Benbow of the 457th FS before opening fire with cannon and machine guns. Benbow's Mustang was last

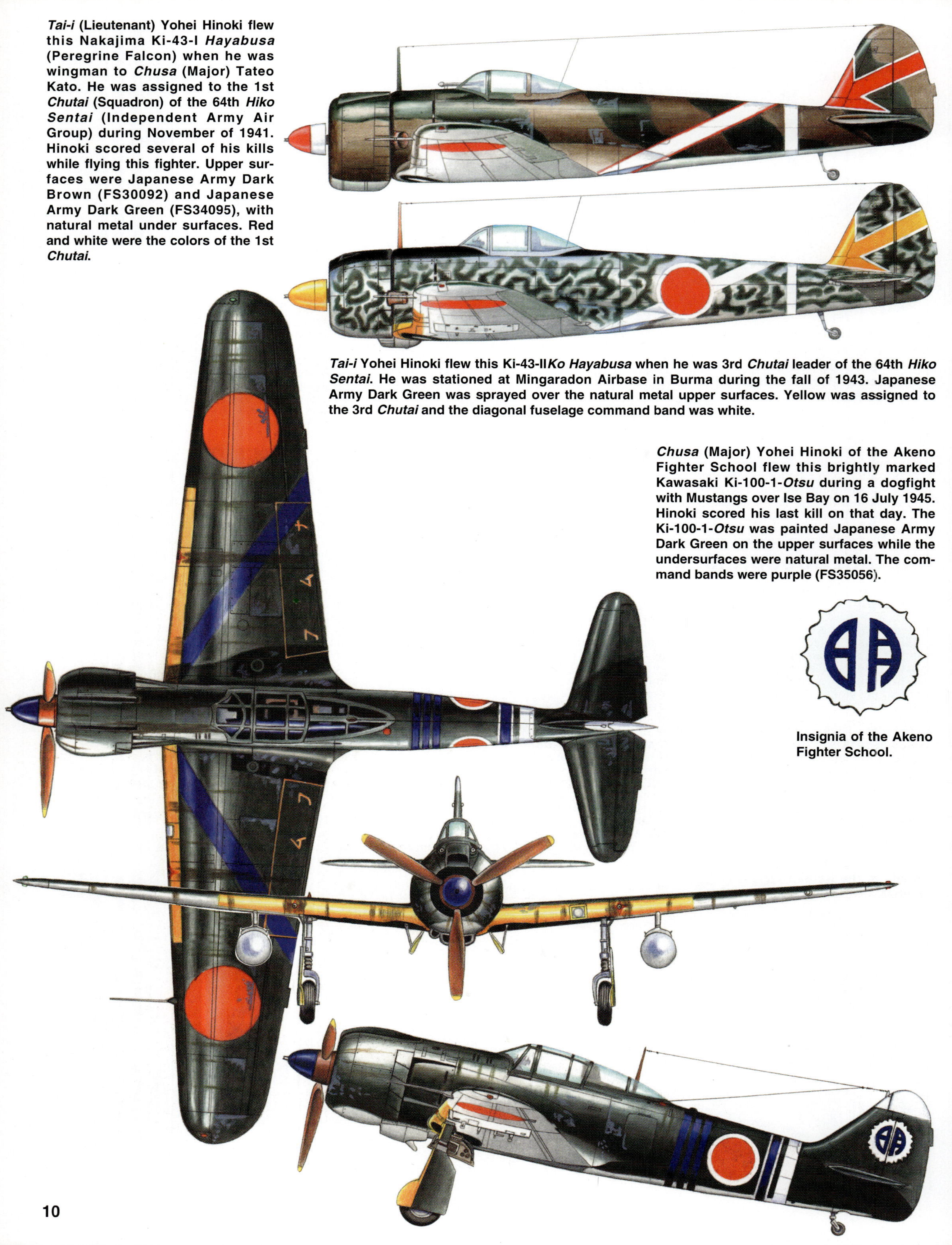

Tai-i (Lieutenant) Yohei Hinoki flew this Nakajima Ki-43-I *Hayabusa* (Peregrine Falcon) when he was wingman to *Chusa* (Major) Tateo Kato. He was assigned to the 1st *Chutai* (Squadron) of the 64th *Hiko Sentai* (Independent Army Air Group) during November of 1941. Hinoki scored several of his kills while flying this fighter. Upper surfaces were Japanese Army Dark Brown (FS30092) and Japanese Army Dark Green (FS34095), with natural metal under surfaces. Red and white were the colors of the 1st *Chutai*.

Tai-i Yohei Hinoki flew this Ki-43-II*Ko Hayabusa* when he was 3rd *Chutai* leader of the 64th *Hiko Sentai*. He was stationed at Mingaradon Airbase in Burma during the fall of 1943. Japanese Army Dark Green was sprayed over the natural metal upper surfaces. Yellow was assigned to the 3rd *Chutai* and the diagonal fuselage command band was white.

Chusa (Major) Yohei Hinoki of the Akeno Fighter School flew this brightly marked Kawasaki Ki-100-1-*Otsu* during a dogfight with Mustangs over Ise Bay on 16 July 1945. Hinoki scored his last kill on that day. The Ki-100-1-*Otsu* was painted Japanese Army Dark Green on the upper surfaces while the undersurfaces were natural metal. The command bands were purple (FS35056).

Insignia of the Akeno Fighter School.

The ace *Jun-i* (Sergeant) Tadao Sumi flew this Kawasaki Ki-61-I-*Hei Hien* (Swallow) of the 2nd *Chutai* (Squadron) of the 244th *Sentai* (Army Air Group). Sumi was stationed at Chofu Airfield near Tokyo in November of 1944. The fighter was overall natural metal with a Medium Red (FS31105) flash across the nose, stripe around the rear fuselage, and stylized 244 on the tail. The propeller and spinner were Red Brown primer (FS30166) and the wing leading edge identification panels were Yellow Ochre (FS33432).

Major Robert W. Moore flew *Stinger VII* (67), a North American P-51D-20 Mustang (44-63483). He was with the 45th FS/15th FG at Iwo Jima's South Field in June of 1945. The Mustang was natural metal overall, with a Green (FS34090) nose and wing and tail stripes. Twelve kill marks are painted under the cockpit. Stripes were on the upper and lower wing surfaces.

Shosa (Captain) Yoshio Yoshida of the 3rd *Chutai*/70th *Sentai* flew this Nakajima Ki-44-II-*Hei Shoki* (Demon) (11). He was stationed at Kashiwa Airfield near Tokyo in June of 1945. The stubby *Shoki* fighter was overall natural metal, with a weathered black anti-glare panel around the cockpit and fuselage number. The tail symbol and wing leading edge identification panels were Yellow Ocher (FS33432). The unique kill marks on the fuselage were stylized maple tree seeds, or samaras, which spin to the ground like many shot-up B-29 heavy bombers went down over Japan during the last months of World War Two. Japanese aces said when the B-29s lost power in one or two engines while carrying a full bomb load they went into uncontrollable spins all the way to the ground.

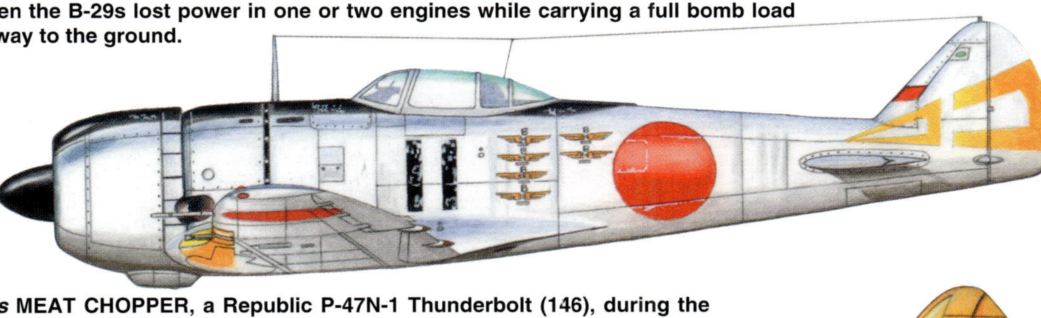

Lieutenant Oscar Perdomo flew *Lil Meaties* MEAT CHOPPER, a Republic P-47N-1 Thunderbolt (146), during the last days of World War Two in August of 1945. Perdomo, who was one of the last aces of the war, was attached to the 464th FS/507th FG, which flew from Ie Shima Island. The Thunderbolt was overall natural metal except for the tail, which was Orange-Yellow (FS33538) with an Insignia Blue (FS35044) stripe.

Lil Meaties MEAT CHOPPER nose art.

Jun-i (Army Sergeant) Nobuji Negishi flew this Kawasaki Ki-45-*Kai Toryu* (Dragon Killer) (White 18) of the 3rd *Chutai*/53rd *Sentai* in November of 1944, when he was stationed at Matsudo Airfield, Japan. The *Toryu* was camouflaged in a dense pattern of Japanese Army Light Gray (FS36492) and Japanese Army Dark Green on the upper surfaces and natural metal undersurfaces. The tail symbol was a stylized 53 in Yellow Ochre (FS33432) for the 53rd *Sentai*. Homeland defense units often had a white background to the red *Hinomaru* (national marking). Propeller hubs were purple (FS35056) and Red-Brown primer (FS30166).

seen trailing smoke in a shallow dive.

Elements of the Akeno Fighter School were formed into the 111th *Sentai* following the engagement of 16 July. Hinoki became the leader of the 2nd *Daitai* (Squadron), which saw little action. *Chusa* (Major) Yohei Hinoki shot down more than 12 enemy aircraft while flying the lightly built and armed *Hayabusa* fighter. This fighter was armed with only two 12.7MM machine guns in the nose cowling. He proved that a skilled and determined pilot in such an outclassed fighter could shoot down Hurricanes, Lightnings, Mustangs, and even Liberators. What Hinoki could have done with a Ki-100 *Goshikisen* or a Ki-84 *Hayate* (Gale) earlier in the war is anyone's guess.

The Ki-43 *Hayabusa* was a lightly built fighter with an 1100 HP radial engine and extremely light wing loading. It climbed well and was highly maneuverable, but it was slow in comparison to Allied fighters like the P-38 Lightning and the P-51 Mustang. Hinoki used the *Hayabusa* to dogfight the British, Australian, and USAAF pilots. In a vertical maneuvering fight, the Japanese fighter held an edge over the heavier Allied fighters and Hinoki was a master at this kind of fighting. He liked to close in to point-blank range before firing which ensured a kill, even with light armament. The Kawasaki Ki-100-1-*Otsu Goshikisen* was a radial-engine version of the Kawasaki Ki-61-1-*Kai Hein* (Swallow) fighter (Allied code name Tony). Late in 1944, there were many *Heins* awaiting inline engines, which could not be delivered due to USAAF bombing. It was decided to mount a 1500 HP radial engine in these fuselages using a German-supplied Fw 190A to demonstrate how to mount a bulky radial engine in a slender fuselage. The resulting Ki-100-1-*Otsu* not only outclassed the original Ki-61, but also could hold its own against the P-51D Mustang and the Vought F4U Corsair and was superior to the Grumman F6F Hellcat. In the hands of a skilled fighter pilot like Yohei Hinoki, the Ki.100-1-*Otsu* was a lethal fighter that could out-climb and out-maneuver the Mustang. The Mustang was faster, but the Ki-100-1-*Otsu* could dive at least as well as the Mustang and Hinoki used this feature to shoot down Benbow's Mustang. Yohei Hinoki, Japan's 'Douglas Bader,' passed away in 1991.

Jun-i (Sergeant) Tadao Sumi

Tadao Sumi was an interesting pilot in many respects. He joined the Imperial Japanese Army (IJA) in the mid-1930s and became an infantryman. He saw ground action during the sieges of Shanghai and Nanking in China before transferring to flight training in February of 1941. The Doolittle Raid on Japan occurred in April of 1942 and Sumi graduated just in time to be assigned to the new 244th *Sentai* assigned to protect the Tokyo area. He later joined the 56th *Sentai*, which was also deployed on home defense.

The Ki-61 *Hien* (Swallow)-equipped 56th *Sentai* did not see action until late 1944, when B-29 Superfortress formations began raiding Japan. Sumi fought against the B-29s on an almost daily basis once these raids began. He became something of a night interception specialist and made repeated attacks on a formation of B-29s over Osaka on the evening of 13 March 1944. Incredibly, Sumi downed four of the heavy bombers and damaged another three. The Ki-61-I-*Hei* Sumi flew that night had approximately the same top speed as an empty B-29, so he apparently lined them up pretty well during his initial attack. He bailed out of the *Hien* as it ran out of gas and struck his shoulder on the fighter's tail. This injury caused him to stay in a hospital for three months.

Tadao Sumi, Ki-61 pilot and victor over B-29 heavy bombers, proudly wears his Bukosho medal on his left chest.

For his action against the tough B-29 bombers, Tadao Sumi was awarded the Bukosho A-Class (the IJA's version of the US Congressional Medal of Honor) on 21 June 1945. He was one of a few men awarded the highest grade of this decoration and became a hero of Japan. Sumi went back into combat and was wounded again, but he ignored the injury and continued to fly. He had shot down five B-29 bombers and damaged four more by the end of World War Two. He had also claimed a P-51 Mustang for a final score of six enemy aircraft shot down. Sumi passed away on 25 July 1985.

Major Robert W. Moore

Robert Moore left Duke University in 1941 to enter flight training with the US Army Air Corps (Army Air Forces from mid-1941). He was commissioned on 5 August 1942 and was immediately sent to Hawaii, where he was assigned to the 78th Fighter Squadron (FS) of the 18th Fighter Group (FG). Moore was transferred to the 45th FS in late November of 1943 and he found himself flying Curtiss P-40N fighters from forward air bases carved out of the jungle in the Gilbert Islands.

Lt. Moore scored his first victory on 26 January 1944, when he downed an A6M3 Zero at low level over Maloelop Atoll. This occurred while escorting B-25 bombers attacking Japanese airbases in the Marshall Islands. Moore then returned to Hawaii, where he was reassigned to the 78th FS and promoted to Captain.

Moore's scoring pace quickened when his squadron received the new long-range P-51 Mustang. The 78th FS was sent to bases on newly-taken Iwo Jima Atoll in early 1945. Moore shot down two A6M5 Zeros over Tokyo while escorting B-29s. He downed a JAAF Ki-43 *Hayabusa* (code name Oscar) over Akenogahara Airfield two weeks after clashing with the Zeros near Tokyo. Following a strafing run on Matsudo Airfield on 25 May 1945, he engaged a large formation of Japanese Naval fighters. Moore shot down two Zeros to become an ace. Rejoining the 45th FS, Moore shot down six more Japanese aircraft by 10 August 1945. He was given command of the 45th FS and stayed with this unit until the war's end, at which time he had 12 victories. He left the service in 1946 and ended up in the oil business in Kentucky.

Shosa (Captain) Yoshio Yoshida

Yoshio Yoshida entered the IJA Officers' Flight Academy in 1939 and graduated in March of 1942. He was then sent to the Akeno Fighter School for additional flight and gunnery training, followed by assignment to the 70th *Sentai* (Army Air Group). This *Sentai* was assigned to protect colonial targets in Anshan, Manchuria from B-29 attack during 1944. Yoshida was flying a Nakajima Ki-44-II-*Hei Shoki* (Demon; Allied code name Tojo) at this time. The stubby *Shoki* had high speed and good climb characteristics. *Tai-i* (Lt.) Yoshida managed to damage a B-29 over Anshan on 8 September 1944.

Stepped up B-29 attacks on the Tokyo area resulted in Yoshida and the 70th *Sentai* being transferred to Kashiwa Airfield in an attempt by the Japanese to protect their Capital. *Shosa* (Captain) Yoshida was given command of the 3rd *Chutai* (Squadron) during heavy fighting in February of 1945. He began training his men in the fine art of downing B-29s by swooping upward from a near-vertical dive and firing at point-blank range into the open bomb bay. This hair-raising method of attack called for split second timing and there was also the hazard of falling bombs and being caught in the explosion as the heavy bomber's load exploded. Yoshida also practiced head-on attacks against the bombers' cockpit and crew, which were similar to those made by *Jagdwaffe* pilots over Germany. He destroyed a B-29 on 13 April and shot another down two days later using the dive and swoop upward method of attack. The *Shokis* were withdrawn at this time and were replaced with the new Nakajima Ki-84-*Ko Hayate* (Gale; Allied code name Frank). This remarkable fighter's top speed exceeded 400 MPH (644 KMH). Burning high quality aviation gasoline in post-war tests, it achieved a top speed of almost 430 MPH (692 KMH) – near that of a P-51D Mustang. Yoshida was in constant combat and claimed another six Superfortresses between 10 March and 25 May. His final score was seven B-29s destroyed with one probable. The IJA rewarded Yoshio Yoshida with the Bukosho (Medal of Honor) for his achievements.

Captain Yoshio Yoshida stands beside his 70th *Sentai* Ki-44-II-*Hei* fighter, with two unique maple seed B-29 kill marks. He received the Bukosho for destroying six B-29s.

Lieutenant Oscar Perdomo

Oscar Perdomo was the last American fighter pilot to make ace during World War Two. He entered the USAAF as an aviation cadet in February of 1943 and earned his wings approximately 11 months later. Perdomo was posted to the 464th FS, 507th FG, which flew the new Republic P-47N Thunderbolt fighters. This fighter was designed for special long-range flights required during the last weeks of World War Two, while US forces closed in on the Japanese home islands. This Thunderbolt variant had a top speed of 460 MPH (740 KMH) and a range with drop tanks exceeding 1500 miles (2414 KM).

The P-47N was the right fighter for the job of taking the war to Korea or the Japanese home islands.

The 507th FG was stationed on Ie Shima Island off Okinawa's west coast. Perdomo was a skilled pilot flying with the 464th FS by the spring of 1945. His Thunderbolt carried the macabre name Lil Meaties MEAT CHOPPER. Combat proved elusive, but on 13 August the 464th FS flew a long-range mission to Keijo, Korea, where they shot down 14 Japanese aircraft. Perdomo claimed four Ki-43 *Hayabusa* fighters during an hour-long chase. Post-war research has shown these kills not to be the light Ki-43s, but the much more lethal Ki-84 (*Hayate* — code name Frank) interceptors. If this was not enough for one mission, he next found a Tachikawa Ki-55 (code name Ida) trainer and downed it with his eight .50 caliber (12.7MM) machine guns, which made him an ace in a day. Two days later, Imperial Japan agreed to surrender and the ceremony was held aboard the battleship USS MISSOURI (BB-63) anchored in Tokyo Bay.

Perdomo left active duty in 1950, but was recalled during the Korean War. He passed away in 1976.

Jun-i (Sergeant) Nobuji Negishi

Nobuji Negishi was born in 1924, entered Tokyo Army Aviation School in October of 1939, and graduated in 1942. He was assigned to the 244th *Sentai* (Army Fighter Group) which was assigned to guard the Tokyo area. He was later assigned to the Japan-based 53rd *Sentai,* which was flying the Kawasaki Ki-45 *Toryu* (Dragon Killer – Allied code name Nick) twin-engine heavy fighter. This fighter was similar to the Luftwaffe's Messerschmitt Bf 110 heavy fighter. The Ki-45 was similar in size to the P-47 Thunderbolt, but its top speed of only 340 MPH (547 KMH) at 20,000 feet (6096 M) made it much slower than its prey, which finally appeared in the form of the B-29 heavy bomber. The only hope pilots of this slow and vulnerable fighter had was its altitude advantage over B-29s. The Ki-45 pilot could either dive through the bomber formation or make a frontal attack. Only one pass could be made, because the *Toryu* lacked sufficient speed to overtake the huge bombers. At night, *Toryu* pilots could zero in on B-29s that were caught in searchlights, but were still at a speed disadvantage. Negishi downed two Superfortress heavy bombers in this manner on 10 March 1945. He learned that slanting 20MM cannons firing upward at a 45° angle was a highly effective weapon at night and destroyed a further four B-29s before the end of World War Two. He was awarded the Bukosho (Medal of Honor) for his successful missions against the B-29 bombers. He ended the war with six Superfortress kills and a further seven damaged bombers.

Major Richard Ira Bong

Dick Bong was the first USAAF ace of World War Two to surpass the 26 kills of World War One ace Eddie Rickenbacker. Joe Foss (28) of the Marine Corps reached the magic number of 26 earlier in the clear skies over Guadalcanal. Bong remains America's top fighter ace with 40 kills notched up in the Southwest Pacific during World War Two and he will be the top ace for some time to come.

Recent wars have not produced the high scores of both world wars. In fact, a Saudi F-15 pilot had the highest score during DESERT STORM with three kills. Bong's score does not compare to those of Erich Hartmann (352) of the Luftwaffe, Hiroyoshi Nishizawa (84) of the Japanese Naval Air Force, or Eino Juutalinin (94) of the Finnish Air Force. This was because Bong was rotated out of combat for propaganda and war bond drive purposes. Most of the other nations, with the exception of the British Empire, left their pilots in combat virtually until they were killed or became top aces. One of the highest scoring aces of the RAF was Johnnie Johnson, who scored 38 kills and was rotated out of combat much like Bong. Oddly, the top scoring Allied ace of World War Two was the Soviet Union's Ivan Kozhedub with 62 kills. The fact is that Bong would have had a higher score if he had been left in combat for a longer period of time.

Dick Bong's father was a Swedish-American and young Richard grew up in upstate Wisconsin. He worked hard and like most farm kids learned how to hunt and – more importantly – to shoot. Duck hunters quickly learn to lead the prey and it is much the same in aerial combat. Like some other aces, Bong joined a government-sponsored civilian pilot training program where he soloed in a Piper Cub and earned his civilian pilots wings.

Enlisting in the Army Air Corps aviation cadet program in May of 1941, Bong completed basic training at Gardner Field, California, then was assigned to Luke Army Air Field, Arizona for advanced pilot training. He earned high marks, especially in gunnery training. Bong was commissioned a month after the United States entered World War Two, but he found himself a gunnery instructor on Lockheed P-38 Lightning fighters, possibly as a result of his high gunnery scores. The normally quiet and almost shy Dick Bong then looped his P-38 around the Golden Gate Bridge in full view of thousands of commuters. His 'punishment,' doled out by General George C. Kenney with a half-hidden grin, was to be sent to the Fifth Air Force, then in Australia! Kenney knew that many squadrons in the Southwest Pacific would receive the P-38, the aircraft Bong had trained in.

Bong was assigned to the 39th Fighter Squadron (FS), 35th Fighter Group (FG) in November of 1942 to gain experience, which was just what he did! He shot down his first two enemy aircraft over New Guinea during December of 1942. While temporarily assigned to the 39th FS, which was equipped with early P-38s, he had become a five-kill ace with several medals. While with his permanent unit, the 9th FS, 49th FG, he notched up nine more kills including A6M3 Zeroes and Ki-43 Oscars. By 14 April 1943, Bong had become a double ace, with most of his kills being singles or doubles. He recorded four victories on 26 July 1943 for a total of 16 kills, which was the Fifth Air Force's best score at the time. Bong was living up to General Kenney's expectations and in fact became a favorite of the general. Bong remained with the 9th FS until November of 1943. With this unit, he was promoted to first lieutenant in April and cap-

Richard Bong talks with his wingman at the time, Thomas Lynch, who scored 20 victories. Bong's P-38 displays 25 kill marks along with a photo of Marge Vattendahl, his fiancée.

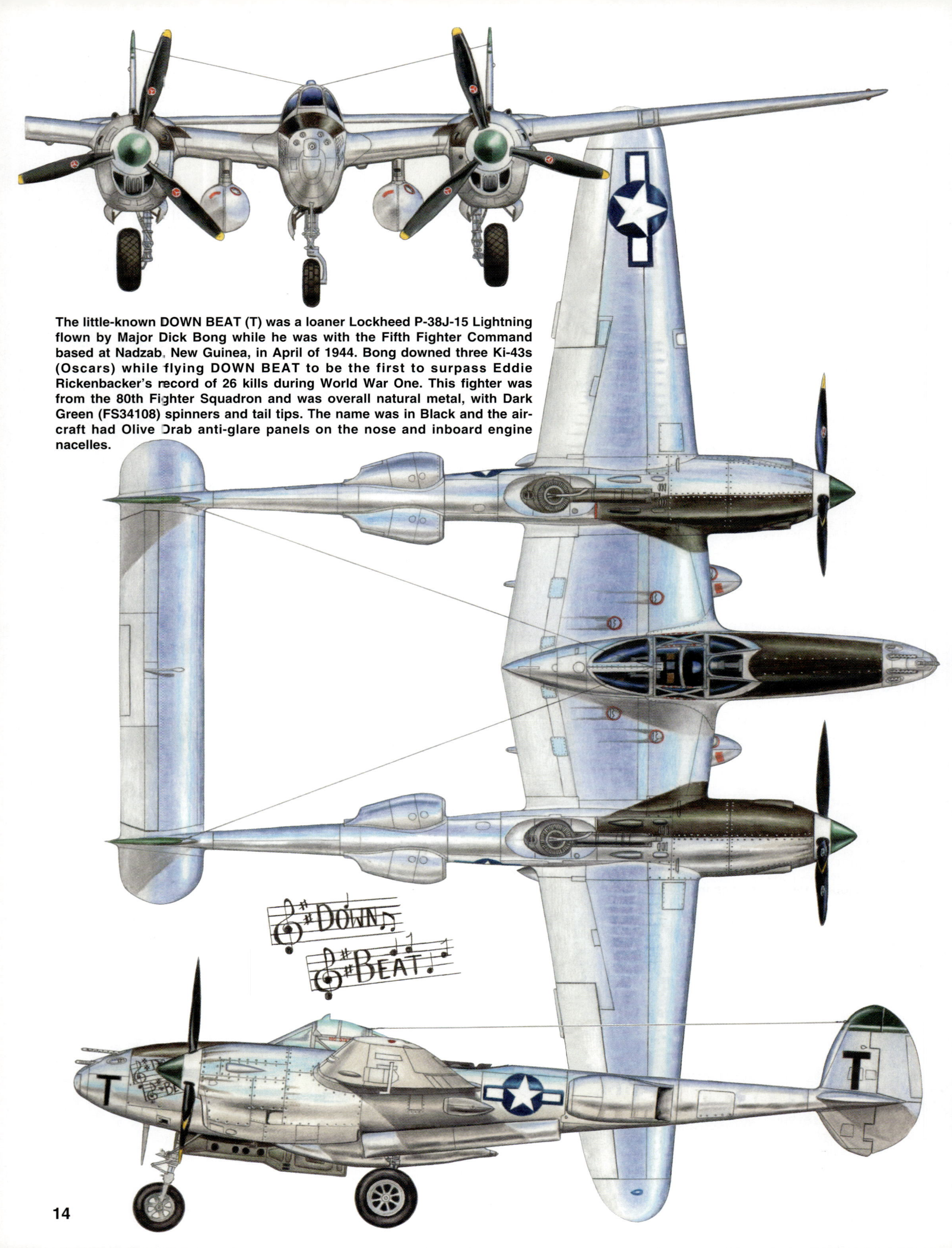

The little-known DOWN BEAT (T) was a loaner Lockheed P-38J-15 Lightning flown by Major Dick Bong while he was with the Fifth Fighter Command based at Nadzab, New Guinea, in April of 1944. Bong downed three Ki-43s (Oscars) while flying DOWN BEAT to be the first to surpass Eddie Rickenbacker's record of 26 kills during World War One. This fighter was from the 80th Fighter Squadron and was overall natural metal, with Dark Green (FS34108) spinners and tail tips. The name was in Black and the aircraft had Olive Drab anti-glare panels on the nose and inboard engine nacelles.

This P-38H Lightning (79) was the first P-38 assigned to Richard Ira 'Dick' Bong while he was attached to the 9th Fighter Squadron. Unlike Bong's later P-38 Lightnings, this one had Olive Drab (FS34087) upper surfaces and Neutral Gray (FS36173) undersurfaces. Spinners were Red (FS11350) and the numbers were white.

This P-38J-15-LO, *Marge* (42-103993), was the most famous of Captain Dick Bong's fighters. He flew this Lightning while with the Fifth Fighter Command stationed at Cape Gloucester in March of 1944. The fighter was overall natural metal and had Red spinners, upper and lower fin tips, and wing tips. Access panels around the gun barrels were also Red. A photograph of Marge Vattendahl, Bong's fiancée, was displayed with Red kill marks on the nose.

This is a close-up of *Marge*'s nose showing the scoreboard and Marge Vattendahl's picture. The author believes this photo was color-tinted rather than black and white.

Major Dick Bong, America's ace of aces, flew this P-38L-1 (42) while with the Fifth Fighter Command stationed at Tacloban, the Philippines in November of 1944. This P-38 was overall natural metal, with Orange-Yellow (FS33538) and Black on the spinners and nose. Anti-glare panels on this P-38 were Black instead of the usual Olive Drab. The scoreboard was painted on the nose below and ahead of the cockpit.

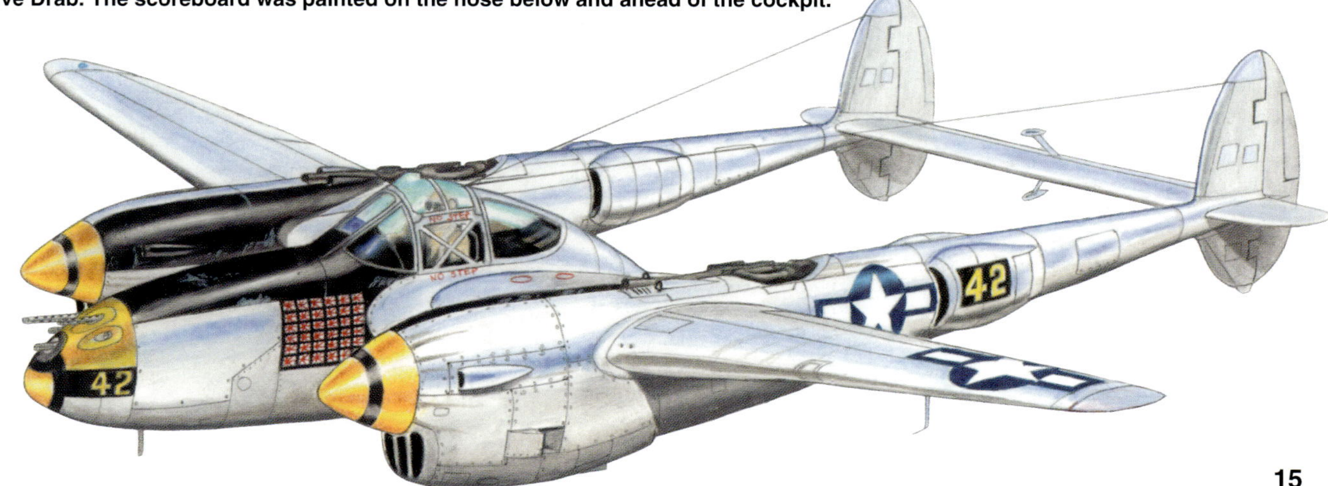

Richard 'Dick' Bong sits in the cockpit of his P-38.

tain in August of that year. Bong was transferred to the Headquarters of V Fighter Command on 11 November, where he was assigned as assistant operations officer in charge of replacement aircraft. This gave Bong an ideal opportunity to continue to fly operational sorties. A brand-new P-38J was assigned for his personal use. He applied a color-tinted photo of Marjorie Vattendahl, his fiancée, on the port side of this fighter. The name *Marge* was painted across the nose in bold, red letters. While flying this shiny fighter on 3 March, Bong shot down two Mitsubishi Ki-21-IIb (Sally) bombers during a sweep over Tadji, New Guinea.

Bong was promoted to Major in April and he was posted to the United States for rest and recuperation after downing three Ki-43 Oscars in combat with the little known DOWN BEAT, a P-38J he had borrowed from the 80th FS. At this time his score was 28, two more than World War One ace Eddie Rickenbacker's tally of 26. He was then reassigned to the Air Force Gunnery School. Bong was known to say that if he had only known as much about aerial gunnery on his first tour as he did when he came out of gunnery school, he might have scored 80 kills. He was not boasting, but he was rather hard on himself. He believed that many Japanese fighters he failed to shoot down escaped mainly because he just did not know enough about the mechanics and art of air-to-air shooting. This showed that even a top-notch deflection shooter like Bong had much to learn about aerial gunnery.

Somehow, Bong managed to pull strings (again with General Kenney's assistance) and returned to the Pacific Theater as a gunnery-training officer in September of 1944. He did not have to enter combat in this position, but he volunteered for an additional 30 operational sorties. While on these missions, he downed 12 more Japanese aircraft to become the top-scoring American pilot with 40 aerial victories. General Kenney recommended his protégé to receive the Congressional Medal of Honor and ordered him to the United States. His value as a hero was far too great to risk him in combat. Major Thomas B. McGuire, Bong's great competition in the 'ace-race,' was killed by determined Imperial Japanese Army pilots on 7 January 1945, forever halting his score at 38. It is also interesting that following the 'Great Marianas Turkey Shoot,' the Naval ace David McCampbell – who destroyed nine Zeros during the afternoon of 24 October 1944 to bring his score to 30 – was briefly tied with Bong. This was not publicized because Bong regained the 'top ace' title three days later. McCampbell ended with 34 enemy aircraft destroyed, number three behind Bong and McGuire.

Bong became a test pilot working with the Lockheed Aircraft Corporation on the new P-80 (later F-80) Shooting Star jet fighter. This aircraft's engine flamed out on takeoff on 6 August 1945. He tried a desperate, low-level bail out, but his parachute failed to open and Richard Ira Bong – hero of America – died at 24 years of age. He had been awarded the Congressional Medal of Honor, the Distinguished Service Cross, two Silver Stars, seven Distinguished Flying Crosses, and 15 Air Medals during his career.

During Major Bong's two tours of combat duty, he had flown 146 combat missions with nearly 400 hours of combat time and had accounted for 40 Japanese aircraft kills. This record was achieved with four P-38 fighters. Bong believed that offense against Japanese fighters always consisted of hit-and-run tactics because the lighter enemy fighters could out-maneuver the heavier P-38 Lightning. He said that any number of Japanese planes could be attacked from above. His advice was, *"Dive on the group, pick a definite plane as your target, and concentrate on him. Pull up in a shallow high speed climb and come back for another pass."* He felt that most enemy fighters could be surprised from the rear and slightly below a large percentage of the time. This confirms that Japanese pilot quality had deteriorated since the beginning of the war. He warned about the 20MM rear guns in Mitsubishi G4M (Betty) and Nakajima Ki-49 (Helen) bombers.

Bong felt the best defense against Japanese fighters was a high-speed dive to approximately 350 MPH (563 KMH), with a 90° right turn thrown in for good measure. The Zeroes and Oscars could not follow such maneuvers because their controls stiffened up in high-speed dives. Bong turned into Japanese attacks whenever he could because the grouped firepower in the P-38's nose was powerful compared to Japanese fighters. Bong always kept his airspeed in combat at 250 MPH (402 KMH) and above as 'good life insurance.' When leading formations against large concentrations of Japanese fighters, Bong always staged flights of P-38s at different elevations as top cover. At least one flight would always be positioned to dive on lower Japanese formations.

Fifth Air Force fighter pilots who flew with Bong believed that the Dick Bong/Thomas J. Lynch team was the hottest combination in the Pacific. No doubt, it was the best Army Air Forces team in the theater. Lynch, with a final score of 20, was one of America's best fighter pilots in his own right. When he teamed with Bong, the results were incredibly destructive to the Japanese.

Bong and Lynch – like the team of Don Gentile (21.83) and John Godfrey (16.33) in the European Theater – would trade the leadership position during fighter missions as if each of them was intuitively flying the other's aircraft as well as his own. This took a high degree of situational awareness on both pilots' parts. They were like men constantly able to read each other's thoughts with the ability to react in a split second to any movement in the air around them. One was always in firing position in battle, while the other kept the shooting aircraft's tail clear. This close teamwork resulted in many kills for Bong and Lynch.

Richard Ira Bong was a good marksman with a flair for deflection shooting. He was a hit-and-run expert with his heavy and less maneuverable P-38 fighters. He had excellent eyesight and when teamed with Thomas Lynch (who also had excellent eyesight), the pair was able to see Japanese formations at great distances. This increased the situational awareness enjoyed by each pilot to the degree that they were able to attack the enemy from the best possible position – from above and out of the sun. Bong was also a great fighter leader and demonstrated that he could lead his stacked formations on fighter missions very destructive to the Japanese. He was soft spoken on the ground, but one of the best 'head-type' fighter pilots in the air.

Richard Bong is America's 'Ace of Aces,' with 40 kills.

Shosa (Captain) Shogo Takeuchi

Shogo Takeuchi was born in Kyoto, Japan in 1918. He graduated from the Army Aviation Academy in September of 1939 and was immediately assigned to the 64th *Sentai* (Army Air Group).

Two of the army's great fighter leaders – *Chusa* (Major) Tateo Kato (18 kills), the 64th *Sentai*'s commanding officer, and *Shosa* Katsumi Anma (32), the 3rd *Chutai* (Squadron) leader – had much to do with Takeuchi's early training. The young Takeuchi developed into a remarkable marksman with superb dog-fighting skills. He was able to show off his skills during a huge dogfight over Singapore on 32 January 1942. His *Chutai* was escorting a formation of Mitsubishi Ki-21 (Allied code name Sally) bombers. The Japanese Ki-43 (code name Oscar) fighters intercepted Hurricane IIs from Nos 232 and 238 Squadrons, which began attacking the bombers. Takeuchi quickly shot down three of the British fighters in full view of his amazed commanding officer, Tateo Kato.

Shogo Takeuchi was the leading Japanese Army Air Force ace over New Guinea, with 30+ victories.

Tai-i (Lieutenant) Shogo Takeuchi transferred to the newly-formed 68th *Sentai*. This unit quickly converted to the new Kawasaki Ki-61 *Hien* (Swallow – code name Tony) fighter. This aircraft – powered by a license-built version of the German Daimler-Benz DB601A in-line engine – was the only liquid-cooled powered Japanese fighter produced during World War Two. It could outrun the USAAF's Curtiss P-40 fighters; however, the Vought F4U Corsair flown by US Navy and Marine squadrons was clearly superior in speed and dive.

The 68th *Sentai* prepared to deploy to New Guinea, where a critical battle with US and Australian forces was building. Takeuchi and his fellow pilots spent several months getting used to the new Ki-61-1 *Hiens* and in December he took over the 2nd *Chutai* as a new *Shosa* (Captain). The 68th *Sentai* arrived at Wewak via Rabaul during June of 1943. The much-vaunted Ki-61 fighter showed its weakness almost immediately in the steamy jungle conditions. Radiator and fuel problems plagued the fighter and reduced its already marginal performance. The *Hien*'s lackluster beginning resulted in low morale among the pilots. Morale improved when five fighters from the 2nd *Chutai* caught and shot down a B-24 heavy bomber over Benabena on 20 July 1943.

Many senior 68th *Sentai* officers were killed in the heavy fighting over New Guinea or were grounded due to tropical illness. Numbers of *Hien* fighters were laid up due to a serious lack of parts. Through all this, Takeuchi flew and led his men by example. He was wounded in combat and was hospitalized for 15 days during October of 1943. Much like later Israeli pilots, he checked himself out of the hospital, declared himself fit to fly, and returned to his base wrapped in bandages. His men cheered as he gently climbed into the cockpit of his Ki-61 fighter with 58 red eagle kill marks on the fuselage.

The 68th *Sentai* had fought until only three pilots and several shot-up Ki-61 fighters were left by December of 1943. When US amphibious forces landed at Arawe Peninsula on the southern end of New Guinea, the Japanese counter-attacked with a bomber raid. Takeuchi and *Chusa* (Major) Kiyoshi Kimura, the *Sentai* commander, led a meager force of Ki-61s. A large group of USAAF P-47 Thunderbolts attacked the Japanese light bombers while they approached the target area. Takeuchi engaged one of the huge Thunderbolts, which was about to shoot down Kimura's *Hien*. During this short action, Takeuchi's fighter took hits and he had to break off. The ace tried to land at Hansa Airfield, but the engine seized and his *Hien* crashed into the trees at the end of runway. Shogo Takeuchi, hero of Japan, died in a fiery crash in the jungles of New Guinea, which he had valiantly tried to defend.

Takeuchi was posthumously promoted to *Chusa* (Major). He had flown some 90 missions over New Guinea and had claimed 16 kills with ten probables. Additionally, he had shot down over 30 enemy aircraft while with the 64th *Sentai* in Burma and Southern China for a total of 46 kills.

Captain Sammy A. Pierce

Future ace Sammy Pierce hailed from Ayden, North Carolina. He graduated from the USAAF flight training program as a staff sergeant pilot on 6 September 1942. He was assigned to the 20th Pursuit Group (PG; later Fighter Group, FG), where he flew P-39D Airacobras, P-40E Warhawks, and Republic P-43 Lancers before being reassigned to the Southwest Pacific. There, he flew P-40E Warhawk fighters with the 8th FS, 49th FG during February of 1942.

Pierce scored his first victory on 11 April 1943, while intercepting a force of G4M (code name Betty) bombers and escorting Zero fighters near Oro Bay, New Guinea. He claimed a Zero destroyed and a Betty bomber probably destroyed. Pierce helped break up a large force of 27 Betty bombers and 48 escorting Zeros over Oro Bay on 14 May. He downed a Zero and a Betty using high side passes in a running fight over the ocean. While flying P-40N Warhawk number 55 on 13 October 1943, he shot down a pair of Aichi D3A (Val) dive-bombers and a Ki-61 (Tony) fighter. These kills came at dusk, but due to lack of confirmation he never received credit for the victories. It appears unusual that naval dive-bombers flew with an army fighter.

Pierce indicated in post-war interviews that the P-40N was lighter and could climb better than the P-40E, but this extra speed came with a price. The P-40N was a *"light-weight, very cheap copy with pretty poor workmanship, poor fittings, clearances and tolerances,"* according to Pierce. It also required much more maintenance than the P-40E. The P-40N could outturn the P-40E, but was still not good enough to mix it up with the Zeros, Oscars, or A6M3s (Hamps). The Imperial Japanese Army *Hien* fighter (code name Tony) could outrun either P-40 model. Pierce said that Japanese fighter pilots did not like to fly head on against the P-40 because of the six wing-mounted .50 caliber (12.7MM) machine guns.

Pierce was injured bailing out of his P-40N on 13 October 1943 and was sent to the US to recuperate. He served as test pilot for a period of time at Wright Field, Ohio and returned to his squadron in the Southwest Pacific, which was now flying P-38 Lightnings. He shot down a Ki-84 *Hayate* (Gale – code name Frank) and two Zeros during an attack on Clark Field in the Philippines while flying a P-38J. Pierce flew with Tom McGuire (38) on this mission and he called it a field day: *"Mainly because the Japanese pilots were about equal to our Cadets in primary training."* Pierce also said that the Frank pilot was the only enemy pilot who knew what he was doing that day. This mission tally is interesting in that the Ki-84 was an army fighter, while the Zeros were naval fighters. There may have been an element of misidentification on Pierce's part. He landed his P-38J without a nose-wheel and completely scrapped it. The next day, his squadron received brand new P-38L-5s, which he said was the best Lightning variant. This was mainly because they had servo boost on the ailerons to give them a good roll rate and dive flaps that could be used for turning. His final score stood at seven victories over Japanese aircraft.

Following World War Two, Pierce served in several US Air Force engineering positions in Texas, England, and Illinois. He retired as a Lieutenant Colonel in October of 1963. He then worked for an industrial machine company and later became project manager of the Northrop F-5 program in Saudi Arabia.

Sammy Pierce sits in the cockpit of one of his P-40s.

Tai-i (Lieutenant) Shogo Takeuchi flew this Nakajima Ki-43-1 *Hayabusa* (Peregrine Falcon, code name Oscar) while with the 64th *Sentai*, 3rd *Chutai* in Malaya during early 1942.

Shosa (Captain) Shogo Takeuchi flew this colorful Ki-61-I-*Otsu Hien* (Swallow; code name Tony) while with the 2nd *Chutai*, 68th *Sentai*. He was stationed at Wewak, New Guinea in October of 1943. The fighter was natural metal, with the upper surfaces sprayed in a pattern of Japanese Army Dark Green (FS34092). The propeller and spinner were Red-Brown primer (FS30166). The 2nd *Chutai* color was red. The 58 red kill marks below the cockpit are wings and represent confirmed as well as probable kills. In this case, they were assigned to the pilot and not the aircraft.

This Curtiss P-40E Warhawk (42) was named KAY STRAWBERRY BLONDE by its pilot, Lieutenant Sammy Pierce of the 8th Fighter Squadron (FS), 49th Fighter Group (FG). He was stationed in New Guinea during early 1943. Colors were faded ANA 612 Medium Green (FS34092) and ANA 616 Sand (FS30279) on the upper surfaces and Light Gray (FS36373) on the undersurfaces. The nose and rudder were painted Red-Orange (FS31302).

Lieutenant Sammy Pierce of the 8th FS flew this P-40N-15 Warhawk (55), named KAY THE STRAWBERRY BLONDE, while stationed in New Guinea in August of 1943. The P-40 is faded Olive Drab (FS34087) over Neutral Gray (FS36173), with a white tail. The Red-Orange stripe around the rear fuselage identified Lt Pierce as a Flight Leader.

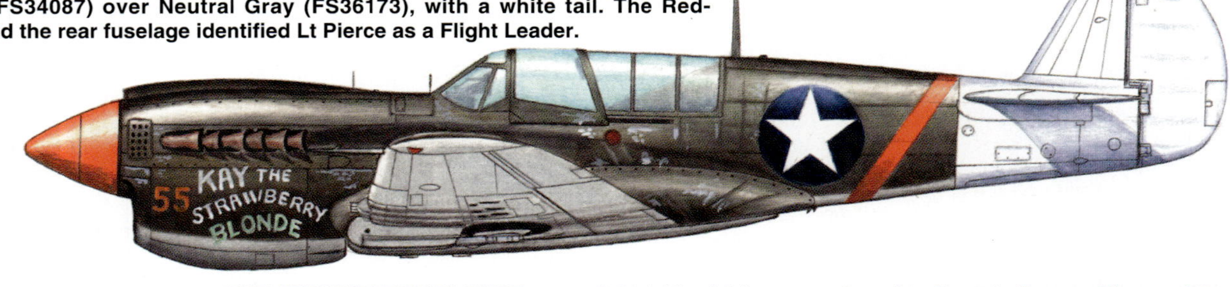

THE STRAWBERRY BLONDE was a P-38J-15, which was assigned to Captain Sammy Pierce of the 8th FS. He shot down three enemy fighters over Clark Field with this P-38. The fighter was overall natural metal with THE STRAWBERRY BLONDE in black letters on the nose. The fighter carried the usual Olive Drab anti-glare panels on the nose and engine nacelles.

made a name for himself with this unit. He was commissioned on 1 August 1917 and received the *Pour le Merite* ('Blue Max') when he had scored 25 victories on 26 November 1917. He was acting commander of *Jasta* 4 and was then made *Staffelführer* (Squadron Leader) on 22 February 1918. Manfred von Richthofen had noticed him by this time and he was assigned to the staff of JG 1 on 16 March 1918. Wusthoff was then given command of *Jasta* 15 in JG 11 on 16 June 1918. One day later, he was shot down while flying ace Georg Hantlemann's (25) Fokker D.VII during a fight with S.E.5A pilots of the RAF. Wounded in both legs, he ended up in French and later German hospitals for almost five years as a result. Finally able to walk unaided, Wusthoff worked for auto manufacturers and finally returned to flying. He crashed and was killed during an aerial exhibition on 18 July 1926, while raising funds for a memorial to Max Immelmann (15).

Wusthoff liked to attack too quickly for von Richthofen's liking and when combined with his blunt personality this got him transferred from JG 1. He thought von Richthofen's tactics were too cautious and sounded off too much about this. He favored hit-and-run tactics and was a good shot. He did well with Albatros D.III and Fokker D.VII fighters because they were fast and could dive well.

Capitano (Captain) Franco Lucchini

Rome native Lucchini attended the *Regia Aeronautica* (Royal Italian Air Force) pilot officer training course in 1935. He received his 'wings' just in time for the Spanish Civil War. Lucchini volunteered for duty in Spain and used the war name 'Lunigiano.' While in Spain, he flew with the *Asso di Bastoni* (Ace of Clubs) XXIII (23) *Gruppo* (Group). Lucchini flew the Fiat CR. 32 biplane fighter, which was a highly maneuverable, but slow fighter. He scored two personal victories and two shared kills. Lucchini was shot down twice and was captured on the second occasion, after which he spent six months in Republican prisons.

When the Spanish Civil War ended in 1939, Lucchini was posted to the elite 4° *Stormo* (Wing), which was located at T2 airfield near the Libyan port of Tobruk. Lucchini was now flying Fiat CR.42 biplane fighters with 90ª *Squadriglia* (Squadron) of the 10° *Gruppo*.

Franco Lucchini flew an assortment of Italian fighters, including the Fiat CR.32, Fiat CR.42, Macchi C.200, and the Macchi C.202. He shot down 26 enemy aircraft, including five kills scored in the Spanish Civil War.

The Fiat CR.42 had the misfortune to be the world's last biplane fighter. It was maneuverable, but slow and was easy prey for modern fighters. The only fighter it could engage with any hope of success was the British Gloster Gladiator, which was also one of the last biplane fighters.

Lucchini scored a shared kill over an RAF Gladiator on 14 June 1940. One week later, he encountered a huge Sunderland I flying boat of No 230 Squadron, which had already been attacked by Italian pilots from 2° *Stormo* and 84ª *Squadriglia*. Lucchini's shooting forced the flying boat to land in the port of Bardia, where the crew was captured. The Sunderland was Lucchini's first personal kill of World War Two, to which he soon added a Gladiator biplane fighter and a Hurricane. Lucchini's 4° *Stormo* was given new Macchi C.200 *Seatta* (Arrow) monoplane fighters and the unit was transferred to Sicily for raids on the nearby British-held island of Malta. He shot down four more Hurricanes while flying the new C.200 between June and September of 1941. A navigational error resulted in Lucchini and several other 4° *Stormo* pilots having to ditch near a small island from which they were later rescued. Lucchini was laid up in a hospital for some time recovering from this accident.

By the time Lucchini was back with 4° *Stormo* in the autumn of 1941, the unit had received the new and deadly Macchi C.202 *Folgore* (Lightning) fighters. While the C.200 was under-powered, slow, and under-armed, the C.202 had a German liquid-cooled engine that gave in a top speed of 370 MPH (595 KMH). It was armed with four heavy machine guns, which gave it more punch than the C.200's two machine guns. This new fighter was equal to the Spitfire Mk V. Lucchini was given command of 84ª *Squadriglia* and after training on the new fighter was back in Sicily participating in bomber escort missions over Malta. He shot down two Spitfire Mk V fighters over the island in May of 1942.

Lucchini and his Folgores were then transferred with the rest of 4° *Stormo* to North Africa. This time they provided air cover for German General Erwin Rommel's summer offensive. Lucchini ensured his 84ª *Squadriglia* was in the center of action, and he claimed four P-40 Kittyhawks, two Spitfires, two Hurricanes, and a Boston (A-20) medium bomber between 4 June and 3 September 1942. He shared in nearly a dozen group victories during this same time period. By 20 October, Lucchini and his fellow pilots were exhausted from being in combat for so long. He managed to shoot down one more P-40, but was himself shot down and badly wounded four days later. He was sent back to Italy on a hospital ship in critical condition.

Lucchini barely survived his wounds and was back with 4° *Stormo* by the spring of 1943, this time commanding the Sicily-based 10° *Gruppo*. The outnumbered Lucchini led his *Folgores* into combat against USAAF B-17 heavy bombers on 5 July 1943. He shot down an escorting Spitfire, but was caught by a defensive cross-fire from the bombers and his C.202 fell out of control. His body was recovered two days later from the tangled remains of his fighter. The *Regia Aeronautica* had lost its second-ranking ace.

Franco Lucchini was always ready to fight and sought out the enemy at every opportunity. His excellent eyesight allowed him to position his men in a favorable location for attack. He was a serious and somewhat timid individual on the ground, but turned into a frightening and aggressive fighter in the air. Lucchini was mentioned twice in the *Bollettino di Guerra* (Dispatches), which was a rare tribute to his bravery in action at the time. During his career, he was decorated with five Silver Medals and one Bronze Medal for bravery. Franco Lucchini was posthumously awarded the Gold Medal for Military Valor following his last action. This Gold Medal is equivalent to the US Congressional Medal of Honor. Franco Lucchini's loss was most grave for both the *Regia Aeronautica* and the entire Italian war effort.

Capitano (Captain) Furio Niclot Doglio

Aeronautical engineer and civil pilot Furio Doglio became a renowned test pilot during the 1930s, when he captured several altitude and speed records. When Italy declared war in 1940, Doglio returned to service as a *Capitano* (Captain) in recognition of his past experience. Initially, he was assigned to 353ª *Squadriglia*, 20° *Gruppo*, 51° *Stormo*, which was part of the ill-fated Italian expedition to Belgium. The 20° *Gruppo* never had a real chance to engage

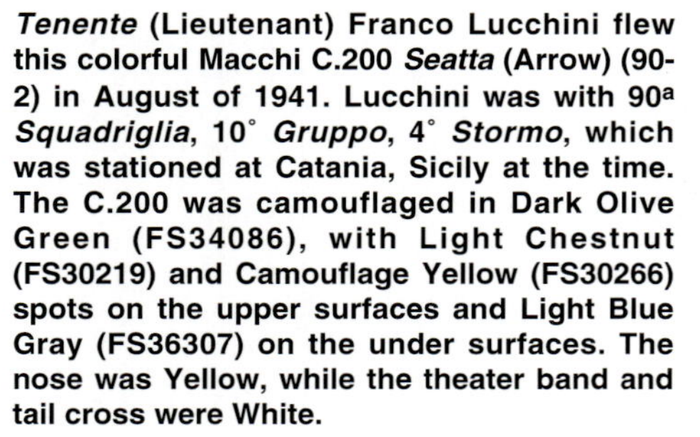

Tenente (Lieutenant) Franco Lucchini flew this colorful Macchi C.200 *Seatta* (Arrow) (90-2) in August of 1941. Lucchini was with 90ª *Squadriglia*, 10° *Gruppo*, 4° *Stormo*, which was stationed at Catania, Sicily at the time. The C.200 was camouflaged in Dark Olive Green (FS34086), with Light Chestnut (FS30219) and Camouflage Yellow (FS30266) spots on the upper surfaces and Light Blue Gray (FS36307) on the under surfaces. The nose was Yellow, while the theater band and tail cross were White.

Red Elephant insignia of the 90ª *Squadriglia*

Capitano (Captain) Franco Lucchini was Commanding Officer (CO) of 84ª *Squadriglia*, 10° *Gruppo*, 4° *Stormo* when he flew this Macchi C.202 *Serie III Folgore* (Lightning) (84-1). He was stationed at Fuka, Sicily during September of 1942. The C.202 was Light Hazel Nut and Dark Olive Green on the upper surfaces and Light Blue Gray on the under surfaces. The nose, wingtips, theater band, and tail cross were White. This fighter was interesting in that the starboard wing had been salvaged from another C.202 and attached to Lucchini's 84-1. The 'smoke-ring' camouflage pattern appears only on the starboard wing.

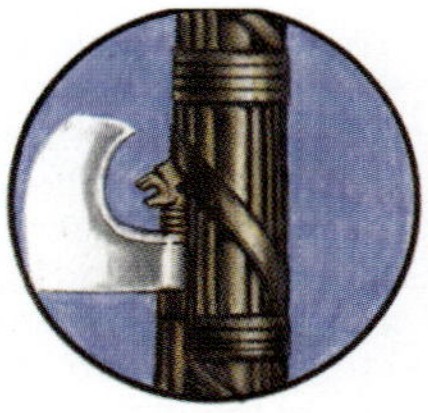

Fasces insignia on fuselage.

Cavallino Rampante (Prancing Horse) insignia of 10° *Gruppo*.

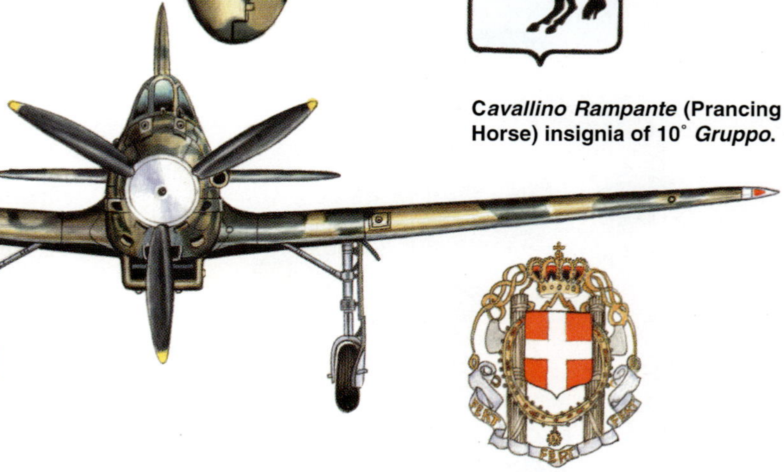

Crest of the House of Savoy, which was painted on the rudder.

F. Baracca was painted in White on 4° *Stormo* fighters. It is the name of World War One ace Francesco Baracca (34).

Capitano (Captain) Furio Niclot Doglio was CO of 151ª *Squadriglia*, 20° *Gruppo*, 51° *Stormo* when he flew this Macchi C.202 *Folgore* (Lightning), *Serie* VII (1-151). He was stationed at Gela, Sicily during July of 1942 and was killed in this fighter over Malta. Colors were Light Chestnut and Dark Olive Green on the upper surfaces over Light Blue Gray under surfaces.

20° *Gruppo* Black Cat and Green Mice insignia.

This Reggiane Re.2001 (150-3) was flown by Malta ace *Tenente* (Lieutenant) Agostino Celentano while stationed at San Pietro di Caltagirone during May of 1942. He was posted to 150ª *Squadriglia*, 2° *Gruppo Autonomo* at the time. Colors were Dark Olive Green on the upper surfaces with Light Blue Gray on the under surfaces. Nose and fuselage bands are White.

2° Gruppo '*Gollettoæ*' Cartoon Crow insignia.

This weary Hawker Hurricane Mk I (Trop) (A/V7474) was flown by two British Malta aces, Flt Lt J. A. Maclachlan and Sgt F. N. Robertson, of No 261 Squadron during November of 1941. Colors were Dark Earth (FS30118) and Middle Stone (FS30266) on the upper surfaces, with a Black port wing undersurface and Sky Blue (FS34504) on the remaining undersurfaces.

Oberleutnant (1st Lt) Gerhard Michalski was *Staffelkapitän* of 4./JG 53 at Pantelleria when he flew this Messerschmitt Bf 109F-4 (White 1). He was the highest scoring German Malta ace, with 26 of his final 73 kills scored there. Colors were RLM 74 Gray-Green (FS34086) and RLM 75 Medium Gray (FS36122) over-sprayed with RLM 71 Dark Green (FS34079) on the upper surfaces, with RLM 65 Light Blue (FS35352) on the undersurfaces. The white fuselage band was painted on all Axis aircraft stationed in the Mediterranean Theater.

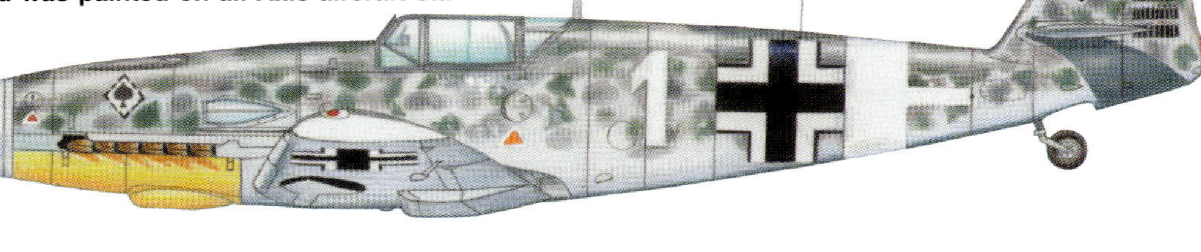

JG 53 Ace of Spades insignia.

This Bf 109E-4 (Yellow 5) was flown by the German Malta ace *Oberleutnant* (1st Lt) Erbo Graf von Kageneck. He was *Staffelkapitän* of 9./JG 27, which was stationed in Sicily during May of 1941. Colors were similar to those on Michalski's fighter without the dark green. The nose was RLM 27 Yellow (FS33637).

in successful combat with the Royal Air Force (RAF) in its Fiat G. 50 fighters over the Channel Front. These fighters were a class below the Spitfire Mk II and would have been on the raw end of the high-speed and high altitude actions being fought over the Channel between the RAF and the Luftwaffe. Doglio did not score during this action; however, he scored his first victory over a Hurricane in North Africa on 30 June 1941.

Doglio was appointed commander of 151ª *Squadriglia*, which returned to Italy to convert to the new Macchi/Castoldi C.202 *Folgore* (Lightning) fighters. These new fighters were Italy's best during World War Two and combined the German DB 605 engine with Italian aerodynamics. It was more than equal to the Spitfire Mk V Doglio encountered over Malta in the weeks to come.

Capitano Doglio scored six victories against Spitfires over Malta between 2 and 13 July 1942. His wingman during the Malta battles was *Maresciallo* (Sergeant) Ennio Tarantola (ten). On 27 July 1942, Doglio engaged Spitfires and misread a hand signal from Tarantola. He continued after a section of RAF fighters ahead of him although he had received the signal to break right. Doglio made a classic error when he did not see another group of Spitfires approaching from his 9 o'clock (directly left) position. Flight Sergeant George Beurling, piloting one of these Spitfire Mk V fighters, fired an accurate deflection shot into the engine of Doglio's C.202, which violently exploded. *Capitano* Furio Niclot Doglio died in a ball of fire at the hands of another ace. Doglio was Buerling's 14th victory out of a total of 31. Buerling downed two Bf 109s and two C.202s on 27 July. The second Italian fighter was Doglio's, Serie VII, 1-151, with the white command pennant under the cockpit.

Capitano Furio Niclot Doglio was posthumously awarded the *Mediglio de Oro* (Gold Medal) for his valor and promoted to the rank of *Maggiore* (major). He held the Silver Medal, two Bronze Medals, and even the German Iron Cross, Second Class at the time of his death over Malta. He was an irreplaceable fighter leader and aviation symbol to young men all over Italy.

Tenente (Lieutenant) Agostino Celentano

Little is known about Agostino Celentano, other than he was one of the few *Regia Aeronautica* (Royal Italian Air Force) fighter pilots to become an ace flying the Reggiane Re.2001 fighter. This aircraft was a radial engine Re.2000 adapted to take the 1175 HP German DB 601A-1 liquid cooled engine. This change gave the fighter a top speed of 337 MPH (542 KMH) at 16,400 feet (4999 M). The Re.2001 was slow, but highly maneuverable in the skies over Malta where the competition was the much faster Spitfire Mk V fighter. *Tenente* Agostino Celentano flew with 150ª *Squadriglia*, 2° *Gruppo Autonomo* (Independent Group), which was one of the few units to receive the Re.2001. Celentano scored six kills over Malta, and had one victory while flying a Fiat G.50 over North Africa in 1941.

Flight Lieutenant J. A. Maclachlan and Sergeant F. N. Robertson

Often when there were fewer fighters than pilots, an aircraft was sometimes flown by more than one ace. Such was the case with Hurricane Mk I (V7474), which was flown by James A. Maclachlan (eight over Malta, 16 total) and Fred N. Robertson (ten over Malta, 11 total). The Hurricane was flown from the British carrier HMS ARGUS to Malta on 17 November 1941. Flying the Hurricane was ex-British Expeditionary Force pilot James Maclachlan. He scored eight kills over Malta before losing an arm in combat during February of 1941. He was later fitted with an artificial limb and scored another eight kills over Europe as a night intruder Hurricane pilot. He was lost over Dieppe, France in July of 1943.

Fred Robertson also flew Hurricane V7474, damaging a CR.42 biplane fighter and destroying a Ju 87 Stuka dive-bomber while flying this fighter. Robertson was an ex-Spitfire pilot who had been transferred to Malta during Operation HURRY. He crashed his first Hurricane when the fighter ran out of fuel while approaching the field at Luqa, Malta. Robertson went on to score ten victories between 20 August 1940 and 23 March 1941. He was Malta's top scoring ace during the first year of the war and was awarded a Distinguished Flying Medal (DFM). Robertson returned to England where he flew night fighters, but did not add to his score. He was killed in a mid-air collision on 31 August 1943.

Hurricane V7474 was finally shot down by a JG 26 Bf 109 on 26 February 1941. Its pilot at the time was C. E. Langdon, a Battle of Britain veteran.

Oberleutnant (1st Lt.) (later *Oberst*–Colonel) Gerhard Michalski

Gerhard Michalski was *Staffelkapitän* (Squadron Commander) of 4./JG 53 when he flew Bf 109F fighters over Malta from December of 1941 until October of 1942. He was stationed at the time on the island of Pantelleria, 120 miles (193 KM) northwest of the British-held island of Malta. Michalski had slowly scored six victories during the Battle of Britain and another 14 kills in Russia before being posted to the Italian airfield on Pantelleria. He went on to become the top German ace over Malta with 26 kills. Michalski was *Kommodore* of JG 4,which was flying the new, long-nose Fw 190D fighters at the end of World War Two. He had scored a total of 73 kills by this time, 14 of them over USAAF heavy bombers. He survived the war, only to die in a car crash some nine months later. It seems that some of the aces had become addicted to speed because many died in automobile or aircraft accidents shortly following the war.

Oberleutnant (1st Lt.) Erbo Graf von Kageneck

Erbo Graf von Kageneck was the *Staffelkapitän* of 9./JG 27 when he flew over Malta. After the German campaign in the Balkans, 9./JG 27 was briefly stationed in Sicily to attack the British-held island of Malta. Kageneck's fighter had a yellow nose left over from Greece and the white rudder and fuselage band of the Mediterranean theater. He is said to have scored several victories over Malta to add to his final score of 67 aerial victories. Following action over Malta, Erbo Graf von Kageneck flew with his *Gruppe* to North Africa, where he scored two of his kills. Australian fighter pilot Clive 'Killer' Caldwell shot Kageneck down on 24 December 1941. Kageneck died of his wounds several days later. Caldwell finished the war with 28 aerial victories.

Gerhard Michalski shows off his scoreboard, which displays 43 kill marks.

Oberleutnant (later *Generaloberst* in World War Two) Ernst Udet

Ernst Udet, Germany's Number Two World War One ace with 62 aerial victories, was a flamboyant and charismatic individual. He had a natural flair for fast motorcycles and aircraft. Udet's career spanned two World Wars, with much barnstorming adventure crammed in between.

Barely 17 years old when World War One broke out, Udet unsuccessfully tried several times to enlist in the Imperial German Army. The army finally accepted him on 21 August 1914. Udet was assigned as a motorcycle messenger to the 26th Wurttemberg Reserves Division. He spent several months in this capacity until he crashed his motorcycle while trying to avoid a shell-hole. After spending ten days in the hospital recovering from his accident, Udet unsuccessfully tried to catch up with his unit in Belgium. While in Liege, he met *Leutnant* von Waxheim, a pilot who had a major impact on the course of Udet's life.

Udet was ordered home, but without hesitation he volunteered for the Pilot's Reserve Detachment in Schliessheim. Like many future aces, he paid for his own pilot training while waiting for orders. Those orders finally came assigning him to pilot training in Darmstadt. Following successful completion of the training, Udet was posted to FA(A) 206 as a *Gefreiter* (Corporal) and was assigned to his observer, *Leutnant* Bruno Justinus. German observers then outranked the pilots and were in charge of the aircraft. He had an exciting break-in period during which he crashed several two-seaters. Udet and Justinus were involved in downing the innovative French pilot Roland Garros (four). At the time, Garros was using deflector blocks attached to the propeller of his Morane scout. This secret device led Anthony Fokker – the Dutch aircraft designer working for the Germans – to design the first successful interrupter gear. This allowed bullets to pass between the propeller blades. This invention dramatically affected the future of air fighting and Udet's own future. For his part in the action, Udet received the Iron Cross Second Class.

Udet was posted to FA 68 (which later became Kek Habsheim) on 18 March 1916. He shot a French Farman F40 out of a formation of 22 while flying his Fokker D.III. Udet was transferred again on 28 September – this time to the fighter unit, Jasta 15. By the end of 1916, he had raised his score to two. His scoring was slow for one who would become a top-scoring ace. He was awarded the Iron Cross First Class and was commissioned as a *Leutnant* (Lieutenant) during January of 1917.

By May of 1917, Udet had shot down six enemy aircraft. He was involved in one of those classic air battles where aces meet in June. Udet met Georges Guynemer who, a month earlier, had knocked down two German fighters in 60 seconds and two more later the same day. The two men circled each other for long minutes, each seeking the lethal advantage. Udet was flying an Albatros D.III, which was larger and heavier than Guynemer's Spad VII and as a result did not turn as well. Udet's twin 7.92MM Spandau machine guns jammed and the great hero of France, perhaps with his own gun jammed, dived for his own lines. Udet felt lucky to be alive because Guynemer had anticipated his every move and had taken evasive action sometimes before Udet made his move. Talk about situational awareness!

He was transferred at his request to *Jasta* 37 on 19 June 1917. Udet became *Jasta* 37's scoring leader approximately five months later, when *Leutnant* Heinrich Gontermann (39) was killed. He raised his score to 15 and was awarded the Knight's Cross with Swords of the Hohenzollern House Order. *Leutnant* Udet became *Jastaführer* (Commanding Officer) of *Jasta* 11 on 23 March 1918. He was awarded the *Pour le Merite* ('Blue Max'), equivalent to the Congressional Medal of Honor, for scoring 20 victories. Udet was invited to join von Richthofen's elite band of fighters, and he accepted the offer. The following day, he was given command of *Jasta* 4, which was equipped with Fokker Dr.I triplanes and later, early OAW-built Fokker D.VII biplane fighters. Udet flew a highly colorful Fokker D.VII with a red fuselage. The top wing had red and white candy stripes while the tail had a white chevron extending along the fuselage sides. Written on the upper tail surface for an attacker from the rear to read was the slogan *Du noch n icht!!* (Not you yet!!). Beginning in 1917, most of his aircraft displayed the LO! marking. Lo was a shortened version of the first name of his fiancée and future wife, Eleonore Zinke.

Udet had 40 kills to his credit when was shot down by a French Breguet's rear gunner. German pilots – unlike their Allied counterparts – were equipped with parachutes at this stage of the war. Udet tried to bail out as his aircraft fell out of the sky, but was horrified to find his parachute hung up on the control column. When he finally broke free, his parachute opened only 300 feet (91 M) from the ground. Udet landed heavily in a shell-hole, after which he was rescued by German infantry.

He raised his score to 60 kills in the heavy fighting over the next two months. Udet was the solid number two German ace behind the fallen Manfred von Richthofen (80). He was awarded the Lübeck Hanseatic Cross and the Hamburg Hanseatic Cross for his actions. Udet had 62 victories when he was badly wounded on 26 September 1918. He was in the hospital recovering from his wounds for the rest of the war.

Udet wandered about Europe after World War One. He tested light aircraft, performed stunt-flying, flew passengers, crashed aircraft for movie makers, raced, and took any work that kept him in the air. He became friends with many of his old enemies, including the American ace of aces, Eddie Rickenbacker. Udet flew all over the world, but was fascinated with the United States. He saw enormous potential in early dive-bombers designed and built in that country, which later influenced the Junkers Ju 87 Stuka. His old war buddy Hermann Göring (22) convinced Udet to join the Luftwaffe when it was formed in 1935. He rose to the rank of *Generaloberst* (Major General) in charge of procurement and new aircraft for the Luftwaffe. Udet's position in the Luftwaffe became untenable due to the political infighting fostered by *Führer* Adolf Hitler and Göring. Ernst Udet – hero of World War One Germany – put a revolver to

Ernst Udet, hero of Germany during World War One, wears the *Pour le Merite* at his throat.

This Albatros D.III (D.1941/16) was flown by *Leutnant* (Lieutenant) Ernst Udet of *Jasta* 15 in January of 1917. The ace was stationed at Kek Habsheim Airfield at the time. The fighter had a Reddish-Brown stained fuselage, with upper wing surfaces in Mauve (FS37160) and Dark Green (FS34258). The rudder was Dark Green, while the undersurfaces were Pale Blue (FS35526).

Leutnant Ernst Udet piloted this Fokker Dr.I (586/17) while he was with *Jasta* 4 in June of 1918. *Leutnant* Hans Kirschstein (27) of *Jasta* 6 (see page 40) first flew this fighter, called the 'Optical Illusion'. *Jasta* 6 gave up its fighters to *Jasta* 4 upon receipt of the new Fokker D.VII. Fuselage, tail surfaces, upper wing, and wheel covers were painted in a dizzying black and white scheme. The nose was Black and the forward fuselage was painted with Olive Brown (FS34064) over doped Natural Fabric (FS33717). Under surfaces were Turquoise (FS34440). LO in Red on the fuselage referred to his fiancée, Eleonore Zinke.

Udet flew Fokker Dr.I (593/17) while with *Jasta* 4. This triplane had a small White LO! inside a square below and to rear of the cockpit. *Jasta* 4 triplanes had cowlings, undersides, and struts painted Turquoise (FS34440), with White tails.

Udet flew this black Albatros D.Va while with *Jasta* 37 during the winter of 1917-1918. At this time his score was 19 kills. This flashy fighter had an all-Black fuselage and wheel covers with a Black and White striped tail. Upper wing surfaces were in the standard four-color lozenge pattern with white stripes. Wing undersurfaces were in the lighter four-color lozenge pattern. LO in White appeared on the fuselage and a White U. was painted on the underside of the port lower wing.

Ernst Udet of *Jasta* 4 flew this early OAW-built Fokker D.VII (2117/18) in August of 1918, while he was stationed at Bernes. This Fokker carried a Black nose along with Black and White fuselage borders. The white LO! was painted over the four-color printed fabric.

Oberleutnant (1st Lt) Ernst Udet flew this BMW-powered Fokker D.VII (4253/18) while commanding officer of *Jasta* 4. Oberleutnant Hermann Göring, who had the rear fuselage and tail painted white, later flew this Fokker. While flown by Udet, colors were Red (FS31120) on the fuselage and the upper surfaces of the stabilizer and elevators. The rudder was White along with a chevron on the upper tail surfaces and the LO! markings. Upper wing surfaces were the dark four-color lozenge camouflage. The light four-color lozenge pattern was used on the undersurfaces.

Oberleutnant Ernst Udet of *Jasta* 4 flew this rare Siemens-Schuckert D.III late in 1918. The fuselage was overpainted in Red and was marked with a White LO! insignia. The wings were left in the standard four-color printed fabric. Udet probably did not score while flying this fighter.

This early Fokker D.VII (526/18) was one of *Leutnant* Ernst Udet's first D.VIIs. This fighter was powered by a 160 HP Mercedes engine. The fuselage was Red, with a White chevron extending along the upper fuselage. The usual White LO! marking was painted on the fuselage sides. The upper wing was candy-striped in Red and White, while the lower wing retained the original dark, four-color lozenge camouflage on its upper surfaces and the light version on the undersurfaces. The slogan *Du doch nicht!!* (Not you yet!!) was painted in White on the upper elevator surfaces. Presumably, enemy pilots on Udet's tail could read this and tremble. Some think that the nose and wheel covers were Black, similar to the OAW-built Fokker above, but this cannot be confirmed.

Ernst Udet sits in the cockpit of a Fokker Dr.I following aerial combat.

his head and committed suicide on 17 September 1941. He was given a lavish state funeral planned by Hermann Göring.

Ernst Udet was a great acrobatic pilot who could coax the most from the late-war BMW-powered Fokker D.VII fighters. These fighters had remarkable climb and high-altitude performance. Udet used this performance to place himself above enemy formations. He was a good hit-and- run specialist, but did not hesitate to dogfight with enemy fighters when the opportunity presented itself. He was also an excellent shot and practiced aerial gunnery all the time. His score rose slowly when flying Albatros fighters and started to increase rapidly when flying Fokker Dr.I and Fokker D.VII fighters. He is known to have flown a red Siemens-Schuckert D.III near the end of World War One and it is not known whether he scored while flying this ultimate, radial engine fighter. The performance of this late war fighter was similar to the British Sopwith Snipe.

Comandante (Commander) Joaquin Garcia-Morato y Castano

Joaquin Garcia-Morato y Castano was already an accomplished pilot and had seen action in Morocco when civil war broke out in Spain in 1936. He had almost 2000 hours in his flight logbook and was an aerobatic champion.

Joaquin Garcia-Morato y Castano was Spain's top-scoring Nationalist ace and the top-scoring ace of the Spanish Civil War.

When war came, he quickly traveled back from vacation in England to Spain. He joined the Nationalist cause led by General Francisco Franco and began aerial operations flying a French-built Nieuport-Delage NiD 52 fighter. He scored his first victory over a Republican Vickers Vildebeeste torpedo-bomber on 12 August 1936. For a time, he flew one of the first German-built Heinkel He 51 fighters and scored victories over a Republican NiD 52 and a French-built Potez 540 bomber on 18 August. He shot down another NiD 52 on 2 September 1936, then switched to an Italian-built Fiat CR.32 biplane fighter, which he flew for the rest of the civil war. He quickly scored his fifth victory, another NiD 52, on 11 September.

Garcia-Morato flew with Italian units for a time to gain experience with this air force. He then formed his own *Patrulla Azul* (Blue Patrol) of three CR.32 fighters. This served as the beginning of much of the Nationalist fighter force. Under Garcia-Morato's leadership, the *Patrulla Azul* developed into an *escuadrilla* (squadron), then a *grupe* (wing), and finally an *escuadra* (division) of two *grupes*. Garcia-Morato shot down six more French-built aircraft and a British-built Hawker Fury during the autumn 1936. On 5 November 1936, he downed another Potez 540 and then he shot down his first Soviet-built I-15.

Garcia-Morato had the opportunity to learn to catch the fast, Soviet-built Tupolev SB-2 medium bombers with his slower CR.32 fighter. On 2 January 1937, he found himself at higher altitude than oncoming SB-2s. He put his CR.32 into a steep dive, which allowed him to catch and down one of these fast bombers. His score stood at 32 kills by mid-1938, but he had been appointed Chief of Operations and could not fly as often. Garcia-Morato managed to test many types of aircraft, including the sleek He 112 and Bf 109B fighters and the Ju 52/3m, He 111, and the Do 17 bombers. Occasionally, he still flew with the *Patrulla Azul* and scored kills over another five fighters and three Polikarpov R-5 attack bombers by 19 January 1939. His score had reached 40 victories, much higher than any other fighter pilot in the Spanish Civil War. Amazingly, all but the first four victories were scored while flying the same CR.32 (fuselage code black 3-51). With the war over at this time, Garcia-Morato flew aerobatics in 3-51 for some reporters. The engine quit during the flight and the Hero of Nationalist Spain, *Comandante* Joaquin Garcia-Morato y Castano, was killed in the crash. What a waste this was!

Garcia-Morato is undoubtedly the top-scorer in CR.32 fighters and had the unique opportunity to fly many early types of fighters and bombers. He fought against a wide variety of French, British, and Soviet-built fighters and bombers. His style was defined by his aerobatic history and by his choice of fighter, the highly maneuverable Fiat CR.32. He liked to mix it up with enemy fighters in swirling dogfights. It is most telling that Garcia-Morato had to dive his slow fighter to catch fast Soviet-built attack bombers. The days of the maneuverable but slow CR.32 were numbered. Fast all-metal monoplanes with speeds approaching and exceeding 400 MPH (644 KMH) would rule the future skies.

American Expatriate Pilot Frank Tinker

Frank Tinker was an American ace in the Spanish Civil War. He was born in Louisiana on 14 July 1909. He graduated from the US Naval Academy in 1933, but was not commissioned until 19 May 1934 due to cost cutting measures. He finally entered flight training and received his wings at Pensacola, Florida. Tinker resigned his commission due to a lack of flying opportunities, then became a mate on an oil tanker in the Gulf of Mexico.

After the Spanish Civil War began in 1936, Frank Tinker had the opportunity to fly fighters. He offered his services as a soldier of fortune to the Spanish Government (the Republican side in the Civil War). Shortly after he arrived in Spain on 3 January 1937, Tinker was assigned to a squadron flying Soviet-built Polikarpov I-15 *Chato* (literally 'flat nose') fighters. His commanding officer was *Capitano* Andres Lacalle, who scored 11 victories.

Tinker flew under the war-name 'Francisco Gomez Trejo' and scored his first kills over two Italian-built CR.32 biplane fighters on 14 and 20 March 1937. He scored again, this time over a German-built Heinkel He 51 on 17 April. Tinker and fellow American Albert (Ajax) Baumler transferred to the Soviet Lakeev Squadron, which flew Polikarpov I-16 monoplane fighters, on 3 May. With this new fighter, called the *Moska* (fly), Tinker claimed two CR.32s during June of 1937, followed by a German-built Bf 109B on 13 July and another Bf 109B four days later. He was the first American to shoot down a Bf 109 fighter. He claimed his eighth and final victory, another CR.32, one day later and finally returned to the United States in August of 1937.

Tinker wrote a book about his experiences during the Spanish Civil War called "Some Still Live," which is a good read to this day.

Frank Tinker was the only American ace of the Spanish Civil War. He scored his kills with the Soviet-built Polikarpov I-16 *Moska* (Fly).

He was shot and killed under mysterious circumstances on 13 June 1939, after he had been accepted to fly for the Chinese Air Force.

Tinker had to use hit-and-run tactics while flying the Polikarpov I-16 fighter against slower but more maneuverable aircraft like the CR.32. This was because the Soviet-built fighter was faster and could dive better than the CR.32; however, the I-16 and the new German-built Bf 109B were approximately equal in speed, climb, and dive. Usually pilots of similar fighters end up in dogfights with the outcome depending on pilot skill. Frank Tinker was an outstanding pilot to have shot down two of these German fighters while flying an I-16.

Wing Commander Robert Stanford Tuck

Robert Stanford Tuck personified the RAF Battle of Britain fighter pilot. He was tall, handsome, carefree, and made a good story for the Times of London. He also was an excellent pilot and a good shot with his Hurricane and Spitfire fighters.

Tuck was born on 1 July 1916 and was educated at St. Dunstan's College. The restless Tuck left school in 1932 to join the Merchant Marine. While on the refrigerator ship MARCONI, he liked to shoot sharks with a rifle and was an outstanding shot, according to reports from that period.

A "Fly with the RAF" newspaper ad caught Tuck's attention while he was on leave from the Merchant Marine in 1935. He soon entered flight training at Uxbridge, England. According to reports, Tuck was a slow starter in training and the future ace and hero of England nearly washed out. He finally soloed and was awarded his pilot wings in August of 1936. He was posted to No 65 Squadron at Hornchurch, England flying Gloster Gladiator I biplane fighters. Tuck maintained his position as his squadron's number one pilot for some time. In the spring of 1939, he was chosen to train on the new Supermarine Spitfire Mark I fighter to become one of the first qualified Spitfire pilots.

Tuck transferred to the Spitfire-equipped No 92 Squadron on 1 May 1940, just in time for the Battle of Britain. On 23 May 1940, Tuck's Squadron flew over the evacuation beach at Dunkirk, France and began patrolling the area in tight, pre-war V-on-V formations that he did not like. Tuck quickly turned into a German attack and opened up at 500 yards (457 M) with his eight .303 caliber (7.7MM) machine guns. He hit the starboard wing of a Bf 109E fighter, which rolled to the left and spiraled down to crash near St. Omer, France. This was Tuck's first kill and he shortly flew back to his field at Hornchurch. Later that afternoon, No 92 Squadron took off once more to patrol Dunkirk. He was soon involved in a huge aerial fight when the British fighters attacked 30 Messerschmitt Bf 110C twin-engine fighters. Tuck quickly shot down one of the heavy and slow German fighters and then chased another on a long dive during which he almost collided with the Bf 110C. The dive quickly ended in a hair-raising chase at low level, skimming over roofs and treetops. At one point, Tuck pulled up to avoid power wires and the German gunner scored some hits on the Spitfire's undersurface. He dropped his nose and fired into the enemy fighter, which crash-landed in an empty field. Tuck circled the wreck and the German pilot shot at him with a pistol, barely missing his head. He returned fire with his eight machine guns and killed the pilot. Tuck had shot down three German fighters during his first day of combat. Upon return to Hornchurch, Tuck found that Squadron Leader Bushell had been shot down over France and he, as the next senior officer, was in temporary command of No 92 Squadron.

When Acting Squadron Leader Tuck led his men to Dunkirk the next day, he did not bunch his Spitfires in tight formation. He opened up the formation to the point where they were 200 feet (61 M) apart. He saw 20 Dornier Do 17 bombers, which were escorted by Bf 110 fighters. The Spitfires took on the bombers, while a Hurricane squadron went after the twin-engine fighters. Tuck locked onto a bomber and shot it down, but not before return-fire wounded him in the leg. He soon had downed another Do 17 over the beach and started the return flight to Hornchurch. When he landed, Tuck found his wound was caused by a metal part from his Spitfire that was loosened by the Do 17 gunner's shot. He was soon patched up and leading more Spitfires. On 2 June, he shot an He 111 medium bomber out of formation and downed an escorting Bf 109E.

Tuck and other RAF pilots participated in comparative tests between a Spitfire Mk II and a captured Bf 109E at Farnborough, England in June of 1940. Tuck said that the Bf 109 was *"without a doubt a most delightful little aeroplane — not as maneuverable as the Spit...but certainly it was slightly faster, and altogether it had a wonderful performance."* Tuck could put himself inside the enemy's cockpit during a dogfight, which added to his ability to shoot down Messerschmitt fighters.

Tuck shot down several more Do 17 and He 111 medium bombers while with No 92 Squadron. On one occasion, he was obliged to bail out of his stricken Spitfire and parachuted onto the Kent estate of Lord Cornwallis, who quickly invited the fighter pilot in for tea and crumpets. Tuck – a veteran of over 1000 hours in Spitfires – was given command of Hurricane I-equipped No 257 Squadron on 11 September 1940. Following his first flight in a Hurricane, he said: *"After the Spit, it was like flying a brick – a great lumbering farmyard stallion compared with a dainty and gentle thoroughbred...It nearly broke my heart, because things seemed tough enough without having to take on 109s in a heavy great kite like this."* The optimist Tuck resolved the problem by saying that the Hurricane did have its values: *"It was a remarkably good gun platform; very steady when you opened fire...It was very easy to fly; had no vices and would take a great deal of punishment and bring you back home...So it was a very fine aircraft for fighter vs. bomber work."*

After minimal training, Tuck found himself leading No 257 Squadron from Debden to intercept bombers approaching London. Tuck tried to get at the bombers, but was forced to engage fighters, shooting down a Bf 110. When a Bar was added to Tuck's Distinguished Flying Cross (DFC), he said that he had just been lucky. Tuck's fortune was renowned in the RAF. He was given a

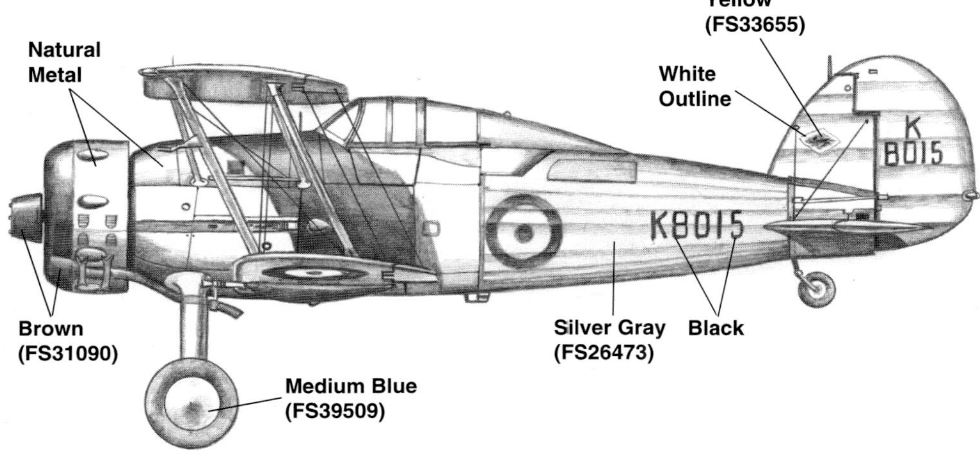

Pilot Officer Robert Stanford Tuck flew this Gloster Gladiator I (K8015) in early 1938. He was assigned to No 65 Squadron at Hornchurch.

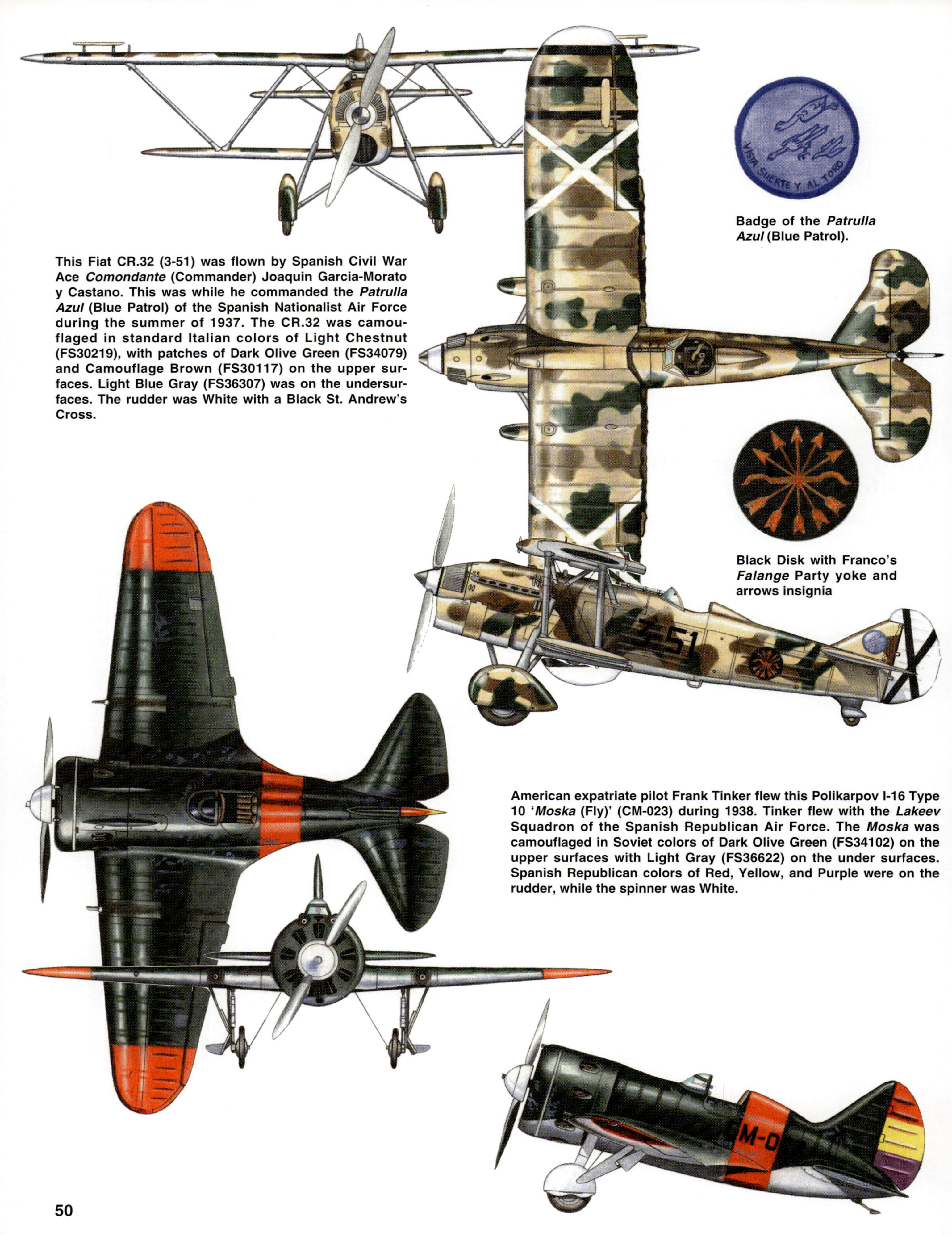

This Fiat CR.32 (3-51) was flown by Spanish Civil War Ace *Comondante* (Commander) Joaquin Garcia-Morato y Castano. This was while he commanded the *Patrulla Azul* (Blue Patrol) of the Spanish Nationalist Air Force during the summer of 1937. The CR.32 was camouflaged in standard Italian colors of Light Chestnut (FS30219), with patches of Dark Olive Green (FS34079) and Camouflage Brown (FS30117) on the upper surfaces. Light Blue Gray (FS36307) was on the undersurfaces. The rudder was White with a Black St. Andrew's Cross.

Badge of the *Patrulla Azul* (Blue Patrol).

Black Disk with Franco's *Falange* Party yoke and arrows insignia

American expatriate pilot Frank Tinker flew this Polikarpov I-16 Type 10 '*Moska* (Fly)' (CM-023) during 1938. Tinker flew with the *Lakeev* Squadron of the Spanish Republican Air Force. The *Moska* was camouflaged in Soviet colors of Dark Olive Green (FS34102) on the upper surfaces with Light Gray (FS36622) on the under surfaces. Spanish Republican colors of Red, Yellow, and Purple were on the rudder, while the spinner was White.

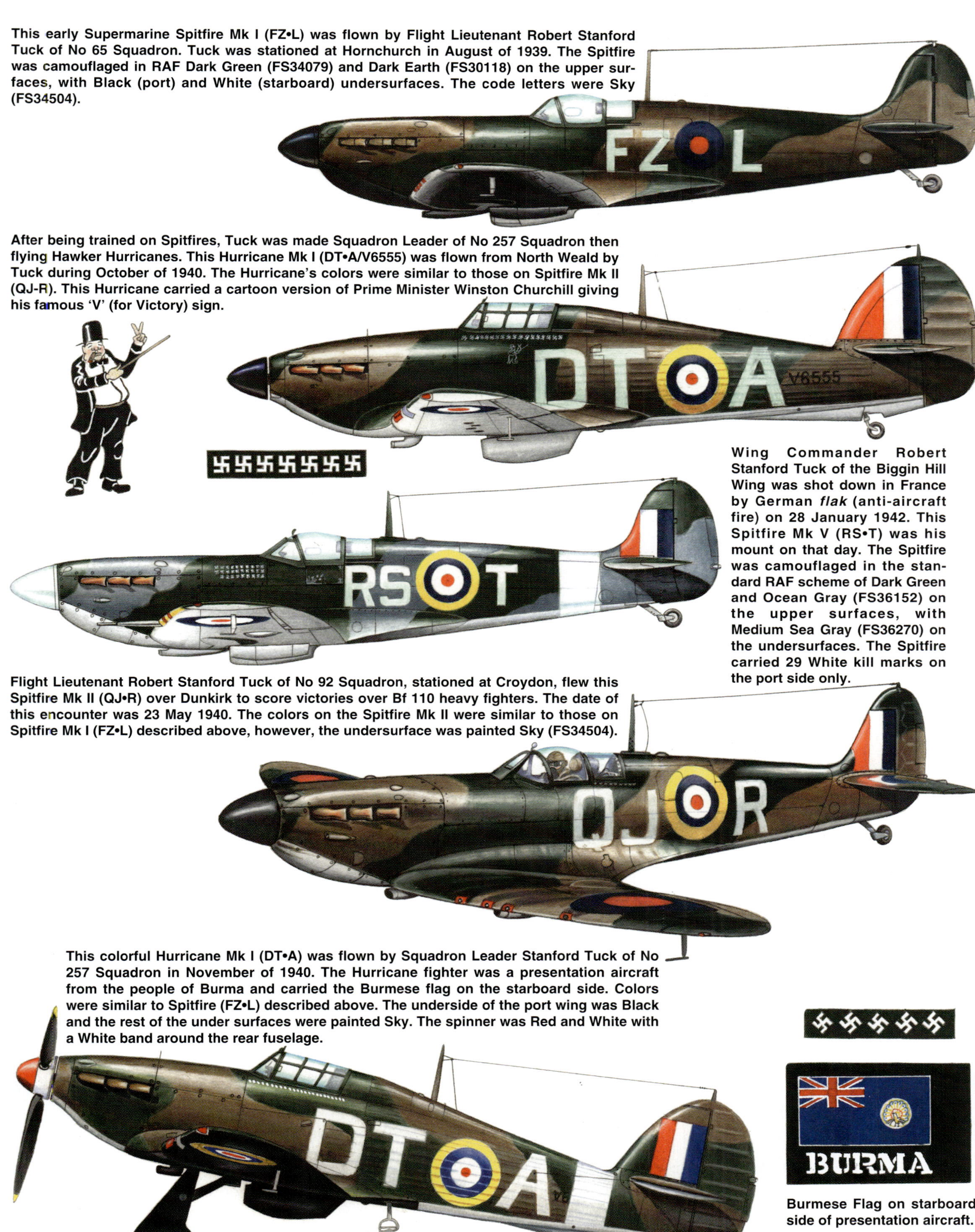

This early Supermarine Spitfire Mk I (FZ•L) was flown by Flight Lieutenant Robert Stanford Tuck of No 65 Squadron. Tuck was stationed at Hornchurch in August of 1939. The Spitfire was camouflaged in RAF Dark Green (FS34079) and Dark Earth (FS30118) on the upper surfaces, with Black (port) and White (starboard) undersurfaces. The code letters were Sky (FS34504).

After being trained on Spitfires, Tuck was made Squadron Leader of No 257 Squadron then flying Hawker Hurricanes. This Hurricane Mk I (DT•A/V6555) was flown from North Weald by Tuck during October of 1940. The Hurricane's colors were similar to those on Spitfire Mk II (QJ-R). This Hurricane carried a cartoon version of Prime Minister Winston Churchill giving his famous 'V' (for Victory) sign.

Wing Commander Robert Stanford Tuck of the Biggin Hill Wing was shot down in France by German *flak* (anti-aircraft fire) on 28 January 1942. This Spitfire Mk V (RS•T) was his mount on that day. The Spitfire was camouflaged in the standard RAF scheme of Dark Green and Ocean Gray (FS36152) on the upper surfaces, with Medium Sea Gray (FS36270) on the undersurfaces. The Spitfire carried 29 White kill marks on the port side only.

Flight Lieutenant Robert Stanford Tuck of No 92 Squadron, stationed at Croydon, flew this Spitfire Mk II (QJ•R) over Dunkirk to score victories over Bf 110 heavy fighters. The date of this encounter was 23 May 1940. The colors on the Spitfire Mk II were similar to those on Spitfire Mk I (FZ•L) described above, however, the undersurface was painted Sky (FS34504).

This colorful Hurricane Mk I (DT•A) was flown by Squadron Leader Stanford Tuck of No 257 Squadron in November of 1940. The Hurricane fighter was a presentation aircraft from the people of Burma and carried the Burmese flag on the starboard side. Colors were similar to Spitfire (FZ•L) described above. The underside of the port wing was Black and the rest of the under surfaces were painted Sky. The spinner was Red and White with a White band around the rear fuselage.

Burmese Flag on starboard side of presentation aircraft.

The British ace Stanford Tuck sits in the cockpit of his Hawker Hurricane. He scored most of his victories during the Battle of Britain.

Distinguished Service Order (DSO) for leading 257 Squadron with great success, outstanding leadership, courage, and skill. The squadron was given the first 20MM cannon-armed Hurricanes at this time. Tuck thought the cannon added killing power to the tired Hurricanes. Following a desperate dogfight with several yellow-nosed Bf 109Es, Tuck was forced to ditch in the sea after shooting down three German fighters with a cannon-armed Hurricane. Tuck was rested after this engagement and relieved of command of No 257 Squadron.

Tuck later took command of the Duxford Wing, which flew American-built Bell P-39 Airacobras, Hawker Mk IA Typhoon fighter-bombers, and Spitfire Mk Vs. Differences between these aircraft hindered operations and Tuck usually flew the Spitfire on missions over France. He was taken off operations in October of 1941, when he and Adolf 'Sailor' Malan (18) toured the United States to share their expertise. Tuck returned to England and took command of the Biggin Hill Wing, which comprised the Spitfire-equipped Numbers 72, 91, 124, and 401 Royal Canadian Air Force (RCAF) squadrons. After leading his two-aircraft formation on a locomotive strafing mission on 28 January 1942, Tuck was shot down in an open field by German 20MM anti-aircraft fire. He was invited soon after he was shot down by *Oberst* (Colonel) Adolph Galland to have dinner with him and his pilots at St. Omer. They compared notes about shooting down each others' wingmen during a Duxford Wing fighter sweep in 1941. After a friendly dinner, Tuck was transferred to the *Dulag Luft* transit camp near Leipzig, Germany. This friendship between Tuck and Galland remained strong until Tuck passed away at age 70 on 5 May 1987. Tuck was involved in the planning for the 'Great Escape,' but was moved from *Stalag Luft* III prison camp to another camp named Belaria. This probably saved Tuck, because the Gestapo (Secret State Police) rounded up and shot virtually all the escapees. Tuck finally escaped at the end of the war to the Russian Front and from there made it back to England. He remained in the RAF until 1949, when he retired to become a mushroom farmer.

Stanford Tuck ended his war with 29 victories and eight probables, making him the eighth-ranked RAF ace. His tactics were to fly in loose pairs, the 'finger four' formation similar to that used by the Luftwaffe. He was quick to get rid of the tight 'V' formations practiced by the pre-war RAF. He liked Spitfires better than Hurricanes, although some of his most famous missions were flown with cannon-armed Hurricanes with No 257 Squadron. Tuck was a good shot and could wring the most out of either the Spitfire or the Hurricane. He favored hit-and-run tactics, but was also good in close fighting. He always turned into enemy attacks, believing this tactic to be the best way to break off attacks.

Flight Lieutenant George Beurling

'Unorthodox,' 'Born Fighter Pilot,' 'Buzz,' and 'Screwball' were all ways to describe the Malta ace George Beurling. In fact, he acquired the nickname 'Screwball' on Malta. He had his own, highly different ways to go after German and Italian fighters and he scored 26 victories in the clear skies over Malta. His final 31 victories make him the top scorer in the Spitfire Mk V. Beurling was Canada's aces of aces and was also number five on the list of British Commonwealth aces.

Single-minded young George could think of nothing but aircraft and flying while growing up in Canada. He did everything possible – including lowering his living expenses to the bare bone – to pay for pilot lessons. Beurling became a bush pilot in the Canadian back country and flew in aerobatic contests where it is said that he easily bested members of the Royal Canadian Air Force (RCAF). Enemies he made at this time by telling them what they did wrong would later emerge when Beurling was 'removed' from the RCAF.

He tried to enlist at age 16 with the Chinese, but was too young. He also tried to join the Finnish Air Force, but his father would not sign the papers. Beurling finally joined the RAF in 1940 and after training was posted to Number 407 Squadron, then flying Spitfire Mk V fighters. He quickly acquired the nickname 'Buzz' for unauthorized low-level acrobatics. Young 'Buzz' shot down two Fw 190A fighters off the French Coast while flying with this unit. He was soon in trouble for leaving the endlessly maneuvering squadron and just going after the enemy and shooting them down.

'Buzz' Beurling hated unnecessary military emphasis on regulations. For this and other reasons, he applied for overseas posting. He ended up with No 249 Squadron stationed at Takali, Malta, which was under round-the-clock siege by the German and Italian air forces. He flew a Spitfire from the aircraft carrier HMS EAGLE to Malta on 9 June 1942. The same day that he arrived on Malta, he was in bone-crushing combat when his squadron intercepted two Axis raids. On 6 July 1942 Beurling was on patrol with other Spitfires when he intercepted three large, three-engine Cant Z-100 bombers, which were being escorted by some 30 Macchi C.200 fighters. He led a hard-hitting attack through the fighter formations and then pulled up at the last minute to fire at the bombers. He damaged a bomber on his first pass and shot down two of the radial-engine C.200s. Beurling shot down three of the new, inline engine Macchi C.202s in one afternoon on 11 July. The new Macchi C.202 had a top speed of 370 MPH (595 KMH), which was faster than the older C.200's top speed of 312 MPH (502 KMH). Beurling's Spitfire Vb with a sand filter had a top speed of 365 MPH (587 KMH). A reluctant George Beurling was given the Distinguished Flying Medal (DFM) for these victories. He was afraid that too much notice would bring promotion to an officer and 'Buzz' Beurling did not think that he was officer material.

He shot down an Re.2001, an Italian fighter with performance similar to a Hurricane, on 18 July. On 27 July, Beurling shot down two C.202s and two Bf 109s. The second C.202 was flown by *Capitano* (Captain) Furio Doglio, who was the Commanding Officer of 151ª *Squadriglia* and an ace with seven Victories (see page 41). Beurling's cannon shells fired from 75° of deflection struck the Italian fighter's engine and the resulting fireball killed Doglio. The Canadian's victory had far-reaching effects within the *Regia Aeronautica* (Royal Italian Air Force), where *Capitano* Doglio had been a great leader and had provided strong leadership.

Beurling shot down 15 enemy aircraft during July of 1942 and was credited with a high strike rate on Malta. He became a de-facto fighter leader over the island because there was action everywhere he was and fellow fighter pilots vicariously used Beurling's situational awareness to find the enemy! Beurling was commissioned an officer that summer, although he doubted his fitness for high rank. He shot 12 enemy aircraft down during September and October of 1942; however, he was wounded in the foot while going to aid another British pilot and was flown back to England for recuperation. On the way back from Malta, Beurling sensed something wrong with the Liberator as it was about to land at Gibraltar and got ready to quickly leave the ailing bomber, which crashed into the Mediterranean Sea just short of the runway. He swam some distance to shore despite a cast on one foot and was one of the few survivors of the crash. Beurling returned to operations in the autumn of 1943 with No 403 Squadron and later with No 412 Squadron, which was flying Spitfire Mk Xs. He scored his last three victories over Fw 190A fighters while with No 412 Squadron.

George Beurling was a complex, maverick character who was also an outstanding fighter pilot, much like Sada-aki Akamatsu (37+) of the Japanese Naval Air Force or the Star of Africa, Hans-Joachim Marseille (158) of the *Jagdwaffe*. His war record saved him from courts martial, much like Akamatsu. He did not smoke or drink and tried not to curse. He used the epithet 'screwball' in place of stronger language so much that it became his nickname while in

Malta. Beurling seemed to live only to fly and fight. He had extremely good eyesight, which he made better with practice, like Saburo Sakai (64), by spotting stars in the daylight and grabbing flies out of the air. By all accounts, there were plenty of these pests on Malta in 1942. Beurling was known to hunt Malta's fast-moving lizard population with a pistol. It is said that he would wait until the lizards were the same size as an enemy fighter at 250 yards (229 M) and then opened fire. He quickly excelled at downing both lizards and enemy fighters.

Flt. Lt. George 'Screwball' Beurling paints another kill mark on his Spitfire Mark V at Takali, Malta in 1942.

Beurling was a loner who preferred to do things his own way and he was an exceptional deflection shot, no doubt from duck hunting as a kid. He was so good at deflection shooting that he could state which part of the enemy aircraft he hit and would later be proved right – down to exactly how many shells struck the target, similar to Hans-Joachim Marseille (158).

Despite all these skills, Beurling was forced out of the RCAF during wartime, perhaps partly as a result of those old enemies he made during the pre-war aerobatic contests! British ace 'Sailor' Malan (18) said: *"He should have been given a long-range Mustang and left alone to fight his private war."* To the author, it is most interesting that the world's air forces tend to weed out aces like Beurling when they should be figuring out how to recruit more of them! The fighter pilot's mission is to shoot down enemy aircraft, which is what Beurling did so well and he was highly vocal about his skills and why prevailing fighter strategy did nothing but waste aviation gasoline. It is said that after Beurling returned from Malta, he was ordered to attend gunnery school. He did so and posted poor accuracy scores. He was asked about why this happened and he replied that he did everything according to what he was taught in the course. He then went through the training course once more and posted perfect scores. He indicated that he used his own theories to achieve these scores and that the prevailing gunnery practice was all wrong!

George Beurling was killed on 20 May 1948, when a Noorduyn Norseman liaison aircraft he was flying from an airport outside Rome crashed after take off. He was on his way to fly Spitfires again – this time for the new state of Israel.

Lieutenant (JG) Joseph D. McGraw

Joseph McGraw grew up in New York and joined the Naval Aviation Cadet program in October of 1942. He was commissioned as a 19-year-old ensign on 16 July 1943, then was assigned to Composite Squadron Ten (VC-10). This squadron and its Eastern Aircraft FM-2 Wildcat fighters embarked on the escort carrier USS GAMBIER BAY (CVE-73) in April of 1944. The tall-tailed FM-2 was a cleaned-up and slightly more powerful version of the earlier Grumman F4F Wildcat. FM-2s were used aboard escort carriers because they were smaller and lighter than the F6F Hellcat, which was in standard US Navy use at this time during World War Two.

McGraw's first victory came when he splashed a Mitsubishi G4M (code name Betty) bomber off Guam on 18 June 1944. During the Battle of Leyte Gulf on 24 October 1944, he shot down two obsolete Kawasaki Ki-48 (Lily) bombers and damaged another that did not go down. The next day, Japanese battleships and cruisers sank GAMBIER BAY off Samar, the Philippines and McGraw flew to the sister ship USS MANILA BAY (CVE-61), where he temporarily joined VC-80. He shot down an Aichi D3A2 Type 99 (Val) dive-bomber and a Mitsubishi A6M3 (Zeke) fighter with VC-80, which made him an ace.

McGraw flew 50 missions in the FM-2 and was shot down on one occasion, ditching near a US destroyer. He was one of only five aces who made all their kills in the FM-2 variant of the obsolete Wildcat. McGraw was an unlikely ace because of the aircraft he flew. Luckily he scored most of his kills against equally obsolete Japanese bombers.

Joseph McGraw was recalled to active duty during the Korean War in 1951. He flew another 80 missions in Grumman F9F Panther jet fighters while assigned to the carrier USS BOXER (CV-21). He scored no further victories and retired from the navy as a Captain in July of 1967. McGraw raised racehorses in Colorado following his naval career.

Tai-i (Lieutenant) Yutaka Morioka

Yutaka Morioka graduated from Etajima (the Japanese equivalent of Annapolis) on 11 November 1941 – just in time for World War Two. He trained as an Aichi D3A2 (code name Val) dive-bomber pilot following graduation, but did not see combat in this aircraft. He was assigned to the Usa *Kokutai* (Naval Air Group) in northern Kyushu as a dive-bomber instructor.

Morioka readily accepted a chance to become a fighter pilot as Japan's war situation became critical. He was transferred from the Usa *Kokutai* to the 302 *Kokutai* at Atsugi, where he began converting to fighters with help from the great Sada-aki Akamatsu (37+ kills). It is said that following one of the first ten-minute mock dogfights, Akamatsu called over the radio: *"Lt Morioka! I have shot you down four times already and I do not want to shoot you down again today – I am already an ace!"* After two months of intense training, the great ace presented Morioka with a fighter pilot diploma.

After conversion, Morioka was given command of three *Chutai* (Squadrons): two with Mitsubishi J2M *Raiden* (Thunderbolt; Allied code name Jack) interceptors, and one with late model Zero fighters. These units were active intercepting B-29 Superfortress heavy bombers over Tokyo and surrounding areas in the war's last days. On one of these flights, a Superfortress rear gunner's lucky shot took off Morioka's left hand. Reportedly, this damaged B-29 was later downed by Morioka's fellow fighter pilots. Following a brief stay in the hospital, he was back as a Zero pilot with an iron claw in place of his left hand. Photos show him manipulating the controls of his fighter with this claw. Morioka led a flight of four Zeros to drive off several US aircraft on 3 August 1945. The Americans were trying to rescue Mustang pilot Captain Edward Mikes, who had been previously shot down. In the ensuing dogfight, Morioka shot down a P-51D Mustang flown by Second Lieutenant John Coneff of the 457th Fighter Squadron. Other Mustangs drove Morioka and his Zeros off, but not before the Japanese strafed Mikes in his raft. Mikes narrowly survived this attack and was eventually rescued by an American submarine.

On 13 August 1945, Morioka managed to down a Consolidated PBY Catalina that was trying to rescue a downed Hellcat pilot in Tokyo Bay. He went on to score his fifth and last aerial victory on 15 August, just two hours before the surrender announcement. Leading a flight of Zeros against six lower flying Hellcats, Morioka managed to put 20MM cannon rounds into a Hellcat, which forced its pilot to bail out. This engagement has been described as the last major dogfight between small and light Zeros and the large and heavy Hellcats in World War Two. Morioka attributed his survival to the famous Sada-aki Akamatsu, who taught him to always turn into opposing fighters and to hold his fire until the enemy filled his windscreen. Morioka became an accountant after the war.

Lieutenant (JG) Frederick J. Streig

Frederick Streig joined the US Navy on 9 January 1942 and completed the naval flight training program at Corpus Christi, Texas in October. He joined Fighting Squadron Seventeen (VF-17), then commanded by Tom Blackburn, which was flying Vought F4U-1 Corsairs. The Corsair had not done well in carrier operations and was being flown exclusively from land bases at this point in World War Two. VF-17 was based on New Georgia Island in the Solomons during late 1943, when Streig caught up with his new unit.

Streig opened his score against the Japanese on 1 November 1943, when he shared credit with another Corsair pilot for an A6M3 (code name Zeke) fighter. Ten days later in the midst of a wild dogfight west of Bougainville, he downed a Ki-61 (code name Tony). He also

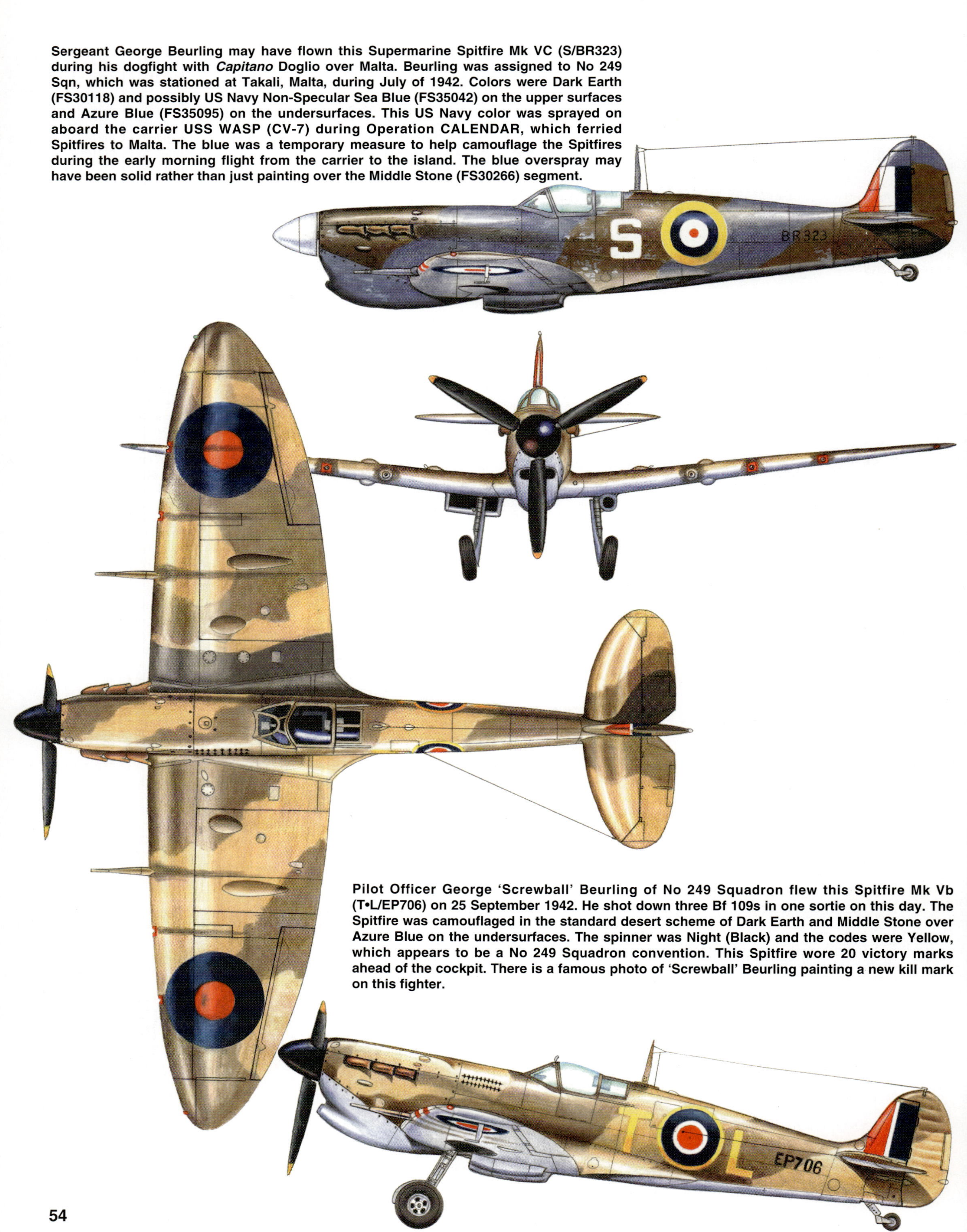

Sergeant George Beurling may have flown this Supermarine Spitfire Mk VC (S/BR323) during his dogfight with *Capitano* Doglio over Malta. Beurling was assigned to No 249 Sqn, which was stationed at Takali, Malta, during July of 1942. Colors were Dark Earth (FS30118) and possibly US Navy Non-Specular Sea Blue (FS35042) on the upper surfaces and Azure Blue (FS35095) on the undersurfaces. This US Navy color was sprayed on aboard the carrier USS WASP (CV-7) during Operation CALENDAR, which ferried Spitfires to Malta. The blue was a temporary measure to help camouflage the Spitfires during the early morning flight from the carrier to the island. The blue overspray may have been solid rather than just painting over the Middle Stone (FS30266) segment.

Pilot Officer George 'Screwball' Beurling of No 249 Squadron flew this Spitfire Mk Vb (T•L/EP706) on 25 September 1942. He shot down three Bf 109s in one sortie on this day. The Spitfire was camouflaged in the standard desert scheme of Dark Earth and Middle Stone over Azure Blue on the undersurfaces. The spinner was Night (Black) and the codes were Yellow, which appears to be a No 249 Squadron convention. This Spitfire wore 20 victory marks ahead of the cockpit. There is a famous photo of 'Screwball' Beurling painting a new kill mark on this fighter.

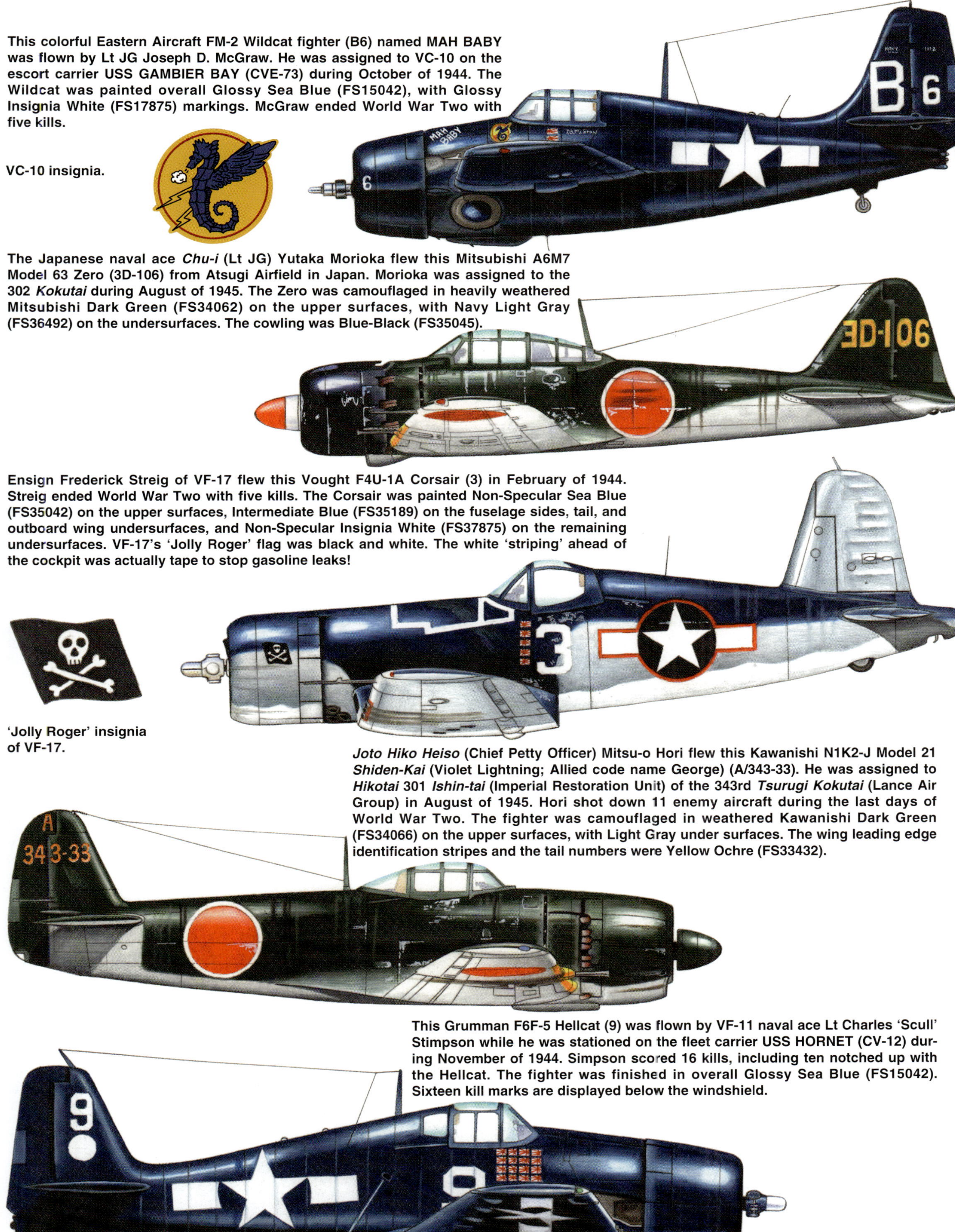

This colorful Eastern Aircraft FM-2 Wildcat fighter (B6) named MAH BABY was flown by Lt JG Joseph D. McGraw. He was assigned to VC-10 on the escort carrier USS GAMBIER BAY (CVE-73) during October of 1944. The Wildcat was painted overall Glossy Sea Blue (FS15042), with Glossy Insignia White (FS17875) markings. McGraw ended World War Two with five kills.

VC-10 insignia.

The Japanese naval ace *Chu-i* (Lt JG) Yutaka Morioka flew this Mitsubishi A6M7 Model 63 Zero (3D-106) from Atsugi Airfield in Japan. Morioka was assigned to the 302 *Kokutai* during August of 1945. The Zero was camouflaged in heavily weathered Mitsubishi Dark Green (FS34062) on the upper surfaces, with Navy Light Gray (FS36492) on the undersurfaces. The cowling was Blue-Black (FS35045).

Ensign Frederick Streig of VF-17 flew this Vought F4U-1A Corsair (3) in February of 1944. Streig ended World War Two with five kills. The Corsair was painted Non-Specular Sea Blue (FS35042) on the upper surfaces, Intermediate Blue (FS35189) on the fuselage sides, tail, and outboard wing undersurfaces, and Non-Specular Insignia White (FS37875) on the remaining undersurfaces. VF-17's 'Jolly Roger' flag was black and white. The white 'striping' ahead of the cockpit was actually tape to stop gasoline leaks!

'Jolly Roger' insignia of VF-17.

Joto Hiko Heiso (Chief Petty Officer) Mitsu-o Hori flew this Kawanishi N1K2-J Model 21 *Shiden-Kai* (Violet Lightning; Allied code name George) (A/343-33). He was assigned to *Hikotai* 301 *Ishin-tai* (Imperial Restoration Unit) of the 343rd *Tsurugi Kokutai* (Lance Air Group) in August of 1945. Hori shot down 11 enemy aircraft during the last days of World War Two. The fighter was camouflaged in weathered Kawanishi Dark Green (FS34066) on the upper surfaces, with Light Gray under surfaces. The wing leading edge identification stripes and the tail numbers were Yellow Ochre (FS33432).

This Grumman F6F-5 Hellcat (9) was flown by VF-11 naval ace Lt Charles 'Scull' Stimpson while he was stationed on the fleet carrier USS HORNET (CV-12) during November of 1944. Simpson scored 16 kills, including ten notched up with the Hellcat. The fighter was finished in overall Glossy Sea Blue (FS15042). Sixteen kill marks are displayed below the windshield.

downed another A6M3 and damaged a Zeke and a Hamp. Some of these mixed claims for Japanese army fighters like the Tony along with a Japanese Navy Zeke seem unusual. The two forces seldom operated together and this coordination weakness resulted in unnecessary losses for the Japanese.

After VF-17 redeployed to Piva Yoke field on Bougainville, Streig shot down two more Zekes over Rabaul, New Britain and shared credit for a third to become an ace. Streig remained in the Navy after World War Two. He served on two carriers, at Naval Air Station (NAS) Pensacola, and was finally nuclear operations officer of Commander-in-Chief Atlantic Fleet (CINCLANT), Western Sea Frontier. He retired from the Navy in July of 1969 with the final grade of Commander. Streig passed away in California in 1995.

Hiko Heisocho (Warrant Officer) Mitsu-o Hori

Mitsu-o Hori was a member of the *Soren* (enlisted) class of student pilots. He completed his flight training course in March of 1942 and was assigned to the Tainan *Kokutai* (Naval Air Group) then stationed at Rabaul. Hori participated in a few intercept missions, but did not score any victories in the Rabaul area. He transferred to the 582nd *Kokutai* and flew convoy protection duty near Lae, New Guinea. Shells from an attacking USAAF P-38 hit Hori's A6M3 Zero during such a mission on 7 January 1943. The wounded Hori managed to bail out and was rescued, after which he was sent to Japan. Unlike some of the older Japanese pilots, he chose to wear a parachute, which saved his life on this occasion.

After recovering from his wounds, Hori served with the Omura *Kokutai* in Japan and then became an instructor with the Ya Hsien *Kokutai* on Hainan Island in the South China Sea. Hori and other instructors helped establish a Zero fighter unit, which they used to attack American bases on the Chinese mainland. Hori shot down a P-40K fighter during one such mission on 15 April 1944, but his Zero was hit and he made a forced landing on Hainan Island.

Following duty as an instructor with the Takao *Kokutai*, he transferred to the 301 Fighter *Hikotai* of the 343rd *Kokutai*. This unit flew the new Kawanishi N1K2-J *Shiden-Kai* (Violet Lightning; Allied code name George) interceptor fighter, of which much was expected. This new fighter was faster and more maneuverable than a Hellcat with a performance envelope similar to an F4U Corsair. Hori scored a further ten kills while flying with *Hikotai* 301. He flew as wingman to *Chusa* (Commander) Naoshi Kanno (25), when the *Hikotai* 301 leader's *Shiden-Kai* suffered an explosion in one of the four wing cannons. Kanno turned down an offer of help from Hori. Following a long dogfight with Corsairs, Hori returned to find Kanno, but the sky over Yakushima was empty. Kanno had been shot down.

Mitsu-o Hori continued to fight air battles over Okinawa and Western Japan until the war ended. He went to work after the war for All Nippon Airways as an airliner captain.

Japanese naval ace Mitsu-o Hori was an 11-kill ace. He was wingman to Naoshi Kanno (25 victories) during the huge air battle when Kanno was killed.

Lieutenant Charles R. Stimpson

Charles 'Scull' Stimpson entered naval flight training immediately following graduation from Santa Barbara State College, California in 1941. His nickname 'Scull' probably referred to his razor-thin features. He received his naval aviator wings on 20 May 1942, after which he quickly found himself flying combat missions in F4F Wildcat fighters on Guadalcanal. Flying from Henderson Field on 16 June 1943, he emerged from a cloud into a formation of Aichi D3A2 Type 99 (Allied code name Val) dive-bombers and shot down four of the obsolete aircraft. He splashed an A6M3 fighter (code name Zeke) on 6 July and another Zeke three days later to end his scoring during his first tour.

Stimpson's unit, VF-11 'Sundowners,' reformed with F6F Hellcats and joined the new carrier USS HORNET (CV-12) in the Admiralty Islands. He participated in the Philippine campaign, the attacks on Formosa (Taiwan) and Okinawa, and the Second Battle of the Philippine Sea. The hunting was outstanding in all those actions. 'Scull' Stimpson, now a Lieutenant, had a good day on 14 October 1944. He and eight other 'Sundowner' pilots were vectored by HORNET's radar into 25 to 30 incoming Japanese fighters and dive-bombers. Stimpson splashed five Zeros and scored hits on two Tonys that he claimed as probables in the swirling dogfight. These 'Tonys' could have been Yokosuka D4Y2 *Suisei* (Comet; code name Judy) dive-bombers, which shared the same liquid-cooled engine with the army Tony fighter. Stimpson destroyed two Japanese Army Ki-43s (code name Oscars) and a Ki-44 (code name Tojo) in the Clark Field area of Luzon, the Philippines on 5 November 1944. He completed his scoring by shooting down a Tony and another Zeke on 14 November. Stimpson scored a total of 16 kills while flying Wildcat and Hellcat naval fighters.

Charles 'Scull' Stimpson was known for multiple victories against a numerically superior enemy and he scored such kills when he met the enemy on four occasions. It did not seem to matter whether he flew obsolete Wildcats or the large and heavy Hellcats, he still scored over Japanese fighters and dive-bombers. He liked to attack enemy formations that outnumbered his own and was an advocate of the 'flock shoot' method, much like the great Japanese ace Sada-aki Akamatsu (37+) over the Japanese home islands in 1945 and Helmut Wick (56) of Germany during the Battle of France. Stimpson would dive into the middle of the Japanese formation, shooting one or two down on the way. The shock and impact would break up the enemy formation, which was just what Stimpson wanted. He could then make pass after pass at scattered enemy aircraft, each time regaining altitude from which he could launch another attack. This was much more dangerous than stalking the enemy in the clouds like all time top ace Eric Hartmann's (352) style, but less so than the attack first and ask questions later style of the German ace Joseph Wurmheller (102), but some pilots ran up high scores using it.

Stimpson served as an instructor at the end of World War Two, but left active duty on 11 October 1945. He remained in the reserves and opened a restaurant in Rancho Santa Fe, California. Stimpson passed away on 20 August 1983. He held the Navy Cross and the Distinguished Flying Cross.

SS-Hauptsturmführer (Captain) Michael Wittmann

Michael Wittmann, who was to become Germany's – and perhaps the world's – greatest Panzer (tank) ace, was born on 22 April 1914 and grew up on a farm in the Oberphalz area in Germany. This early farm life turned out to be highly important to his future because young Wittmann learned how to maintain and operate tractors and other farm equipment. Tanks got their start as armored tractors during World War One. Wittmann joined the *Reichs Arbeitdienst* (Voluntary Labor Service) at age 19 and shortly after enlisted in the regular German Army (*Wehrmacht*) on 30 October 1934, when he turned 20. He was assigned to the 10th Company of the 19th Infantry Regiment. Finding that he did well in military service, Wittmann applied for membership in the *Allgemeine-SS* (General SS) and was sent to SS school in Berlin on 1 April 1937. He was assigned to the *Waffen-SS* (Armed-SS) at this time and became a sworn member of the *SS-Leibstandarte Adolf Hitler* (LAH; Bodyguard Adolf Hitler) Division. Wittmann was a driver of a Sd.Kfz.222 light armored car by the outbreak of World War Two. He was in continuous combat

Michael Wittmann poses after receiving the Oak Leaves to the Knight's Cross for bravery and leadership on the Russian Front. He wears the uniform of an *SS-Obersturmführer* (1st Lieutenant).

from the invasion of Poland on 1 September 1939 to his death on 9 August 1944.

During the Battle of France in 1940, *SS-Untersharführer* (Sergeant) Michael Wittmann commanded an Sd.Kfz.222 light armored car and carried out reconnaissance duties for the LAH. The LAH was transferred to the Balkans in 1941 to assist the Royal Italian Army in conquering Greece, which was not going well for the Italians at the time. His superior record resulted in Wittmann being given command of a new *Sturmgeshutz* (StuG) III Ausf. A assault gun. This was a *Panzerkampfwagen* (PzKpfw) III tank chassis without a turret that mounted a short 7.5 CM L/24 gun. The StuG III was used as mobile artillery and later as ambush tank killers.

Wittmann and the LAH crossed into southern Russia at the beginning of Operation BARBAROSSA on 22 June 1941. Ten days later, Wittmann was awarded the Iron Cross 2nd Class for bravery in the face of the enemy after heavy fighting. He had started his career as a famous destroyer of enemy tanks. Wittmann was wounded twice by shrapnel hitting his StuG III and was awarded wound badges and the Iron Cross 1st Class for bravery. He was sent to officer cadet school on 8 October 1941, which turned out to be one of the best decisions the *Waffen-SS* leadership made during the war.

Wittmann was commissioned as an *SS-Untersturmführer* (2nd Lt.) upon his graduation from the SS school at Bad Tolz on 12 December 1942. He was extensively trained during the next several months to be commander of the new PzKpfw VI Tiger I heavy tank. Wittmann and his Tiger I crew (gunner Balthasar Woll, loader Kurt Berges, driver Gustl Kirschner, and radio operator Herbert Pollmann) rejoined the LAH in Russia. They went on to destroy 30 Soviet T-34/76 tanks and 28 anti-tank guns around Belgorod during the first few days of the Battle of Kursk, which began on 5 July 1943. During this battle, the Soviet tank commanders found they had to close within suicidal ranges for the T-34's weak main gun to be able to penetrate the Tiger's thick armor. Wittmann understood that the best defense against determined attack was to turn into the attack with a quick counter attack – not unlike strategy used by top aces in aerial combat. This exposed only the heavily armored front of his Tiger I. The shock of some of Wittmann's attacks scattered the enemy so his famous gunner Balthasar 'Bobby' Woll could knock them out almost at his leisure. Wittmann certainly used the 'flock shoot' method as well as many of his aerial counterparts.

On 7 July 1943, Wittmann and his now famous Tiger I crew destroyed another seven T-34 tanks and 19 guns of the Soviet 29th Anti-Tank Gun Brigade at Teterevino and Oboyan. Wittmann and his crew then almost single-handedly drove off a Soviet counter attack of over 60 tanks. They later destroyed the Soviet 181st Tank Brigade as a fighting unit. Following this action, the LAH was ordered to Italy to perform anti-partisan duties and to get much needed rest and time to rebuild. Once this rebuilding was complete, the LAH was ordered back to Russia, where the German troops were forced to take the defensive. The Tiger I was better on defense – due to its high velocity 8.8 CM KwK 36 L/56 main gun – than it was on offense, because it was not as maneuverable as the smaller Soviet tanks of the time. The LAH commanders formed two, and later three, battle groups for defensive actions.

Wittmann and his Tiger crew destroyed six Soviet T-34/76 tanks and five anti-tank guns on the morning of 21 November 1943. After rearming and refueling their Tiger I, they destroyed ten more enemy tanks and seven anti-tank guns near Brusilov and Fastov. Wittmann was now beginning to be able to read the terrain, figure out the enemy intentions, and then force his personal style onto the battlefield. The enemy was forced to fight his way and was annihilated. Wittmann's tank and crew intercepted and destroyed an entire convoy of soft-skin transport vehicles and their tank escort on a snow-covered road near Styrty on 4 December 1943. Wittmann destroyed his 60th tank two days later in fierce action near Golovin, Russia, followed by six of the up-gunned T-34/85 tanks on 9 January 1944. They scored their 88th tank kill during fighting between Kortyky and Styrty on 14 January. It was typical that Michael Wittmann would not accept the offered Knight's Cross until his gunner 'Bobby' Woll was given the same award. This was unheard of, as this high award was reserved for the officer corps rather than brave men in the enlisted ranks. Unit commander *SS-Sturmbannführer* (Major) Joachim Peiper of later Battle of the Bulge fame presented the Knight's Cross to both men and the Iron Cross First Class to the rest of the tank crew. They posed in front of their whitewashed Tiger I with 88 kill marks on the gun barrel in photographs taken on 14 January. Later the same day, Wittmann and his crew destroyed 19 more Soviet tanks and shot up three super heavy self-propelled guns!

Wittmann was awarded the Oak Leaves to his Knight's Cross for his meritorious service and was promoted to *SS-Obersturmführer* (1st Lt.) on 30 January. With no let up in sight, Wittmann and his famous crew destroyed nine more Soviet tanks during an attack on Boyarka. They scored kills over 13 enemy self-propelled guns on 10 February 1944. At this point in time, Michael Wittmann had 119 tank kills to his credit. He was scoring difficult tank kills at a similar rate to which many Luftwaffe fighter pilots were shooting down Soviet aircraft. On 15 February 1944, Wittmann was given command of 2 Company *s SS-Panzer Abt.* (SS Tank Battalion) 101. The small *s* in front of SS stood for *schwere* (heavy), which referred to the Tiger I heavy tanks. Many LAH tanks of this time period were marked with mixed letters and numbers on their turrets, as was Wittmann's Tiger S05 (*Schwere* 05 or *Stab* 05). Following the hair-raising action in Russia, the beleaguered LAH was assigned to the Western Front, where they would rest, regroup, and train in France and Belgium.

During a short home leave, Wittmann married Hildegard Burmester on 1 March 1944. Two weeks later, he delivered a pep talk to workers at the Henschel tank factory where Tiger I tanks were being manufactured.

Shortly after the D-Day landing at Normandy on 6 June, Wittmann was ordered to move his battle group toward the fighting. Many excellent photos show Wittmann standing in the hatch of his Tiger Red 205 along with his column of camouflaged Tiger tanks as they moved over French roads. They were attacked at one point by Allied fighter bombers and some tanks were damaged and had to be left behind with their crews. Although 'Bobby' Woll was now a tank commander, Wittmann took him forward as his gunner, just as it was in Russia. Damage and breakdowns forced Wittmann to order a halt for needed repairs on 12 June. They had to hide the tanks by day and travel at night to avoid Allied air cover. Thinner armor atop the tanks made them vulnerable to rockets fired by marauding Typhoon and P-47 Thunderbolt fighter bombers.

By 13 June, Wittmann and some of his tank force were guarding the left flank of the *Panzer Lehr* Division near Villers-Bocage, southwest of Caen, France – the objective of Allied fighting. British General Sir Bernard Montgomery sent the 22nd Armored Brigade of the 7th Armored Division in a wide flanking movement. This was planned to meet up with a similar

The Tiger ace Michael Wittmann wears a battered 'mission cap.'

SS-Unterscharführer (Sergeant) Michael Wittmann commanded this Sd.Kfz.222 *Spähwagen* (Light Reconnaissance Armored Car) of the *SS-Leibstandarte Adolf Hitler* (LAH; Bodyguard Adolf Hitler) Division on the morning of 10 May 1940. This was the first day of the Battle for France. The *Spähwagen* was painted overall Panzer Gray (FS36099), with a light coat of brown dust. LAH vehicles were always marked with a white shield and key, which were the Division's symbols. Early LAH vehicles were also marked with a white bull's-eye somewhere on the front. Two circles indicated the second company and one circle stood for the first company. The Sd.Kfz.222 carried a crew of three and was armed with a 20MM KwK 30 cannon and a 7.92MM MG-34 machine gun plus MP-40 machine pistols. Bug-like 'feelers' mounted on the fenders allowed the driver to avoid nearby obstructions.

LAH key and shield insignia.

LAH Second Company Vehicle Insignia

SS-Unterscharführer (Sergeant) Michael Wittmann commanded this *Sturmgeschutz* (StuG) III Ausf. A assault gun during the early battles of Operation BARBAROSSA in Russia. The StuG III was painted overall Panzer Gray, with a light coat of brown dust. Like the Sd.Kfz.222, the StuG III carried a white circle (first company) on the front of the vehicle. It is marked with the early, narrow white cross national insignia. The white LAH key does not show up in the existing photos, but is probably on the StuG III's rear and possibly covered by dust.

This famous and controversial PzKpfw VI Ausf H/E, Tiger I was a backdrop for photos of *SS-Untersturmführer* (2nd Lt.) Michael Wittmann and his crew receiving medals from *SS-Sturmbannführer* (Major) Joachim Peiper at Berdichev, Russia on 14 January 1944. The early Tiger I was overall Panzer Yellow (FS33434), with a coat of temporary White paint applied over the top of the original color that is showing through due to wear. The author has studied available photos and has concluded that the Tiger was numbered S05 and was possibly a *Stab* or headquarters tank. This has led to speculation that the tank happened to be available for the medal ceremony and was not assigned to Wittmann. It is also possible that the turret number stood for *Schwere* (heavy tank) 05. Wittmann's 88 kill marks appear on the barrel of the KwK 36 L/56 8.8 CM main gun. These kill marks, like the turret number, appear to have been rubbed through the white paint to show the Panzer Yellow and then touched up with White. This Tiger I possibly could have been Wittmann's tank. The LAH shield, key, and oak leaves insignia are painted on the tank's front left side.

SS-Obersturmführer (1st Lt.) Michael Wittmann used this late model PzKpfw VI Ausf. H/E Tiger I (Red 205) when he commanded the Second Company of *Schwere SS-Panzer-Abteilung* 101. This was prior to and during the first part of the famous tank battle in Villers-Bocage, France, on 13 June 1944. The Tiger I was camouflaged in a scheme of Panzer Yellow, Olive Green (FS34089), and Red Brown (FS32169). Only the sides and front of the tank were covered in *Zimmerit* (the plaster-based, anti-magnetic coating).

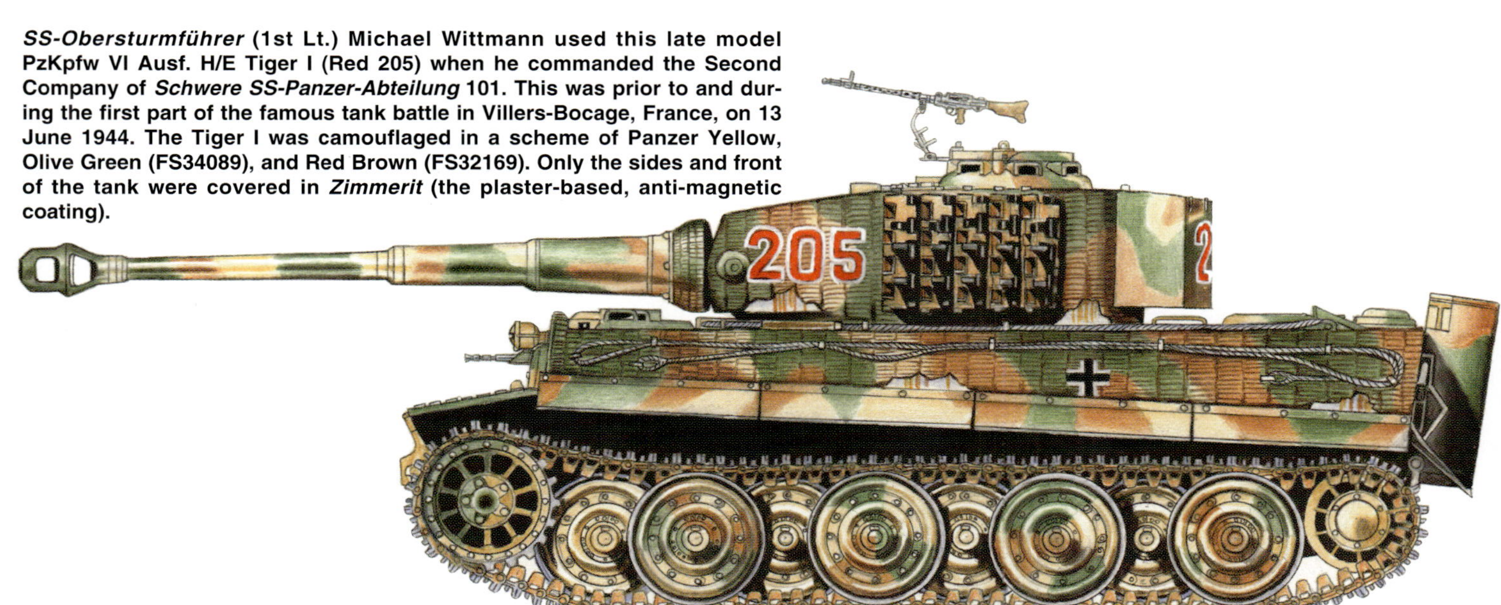

SS-Obersturmführer Michael Wittmann used this Tiger (Red 222) during his second trip through Villers-Bocage on 13 June 1944. Panzer aces like Wittmann always had a spare tank and following his first trip through Villers-Bocage, his Tiger I (Red 205) was low on fuel and out of ammunition. He simply commandeered Tiger 222 from *SS-Untersharführer* Kurt Sowa, which was full of fuel and ammunition. This tank was disabled following a hit in the track from a 6-pounder anti-tank gun of the British Queens Regiment firing from cover of a building. Wittmann and his crew escaped unharmed and the lightly damaged tank was later recovered. This Tiger I was camouflaged in colors similar to Wittmann's number 205.

LAH shield with crossed keys and oak leaves.

SS-Hauptsturmführer (Captain) Michael Wittmann was killed in this Tiger (White 007) during furious fighting at St Aignan-de-Cramesnil near the 'Falaise Pocket' on 8 August 1944. It is believed that Wittmann's last Tiger tank was knocked out by a rocket-firing Typhoon fighter-bomber. This Tiger I was a *Stab* (Headquarters) command tank and was originally assigned to *SS-Standartenführer* (Colonel) von Westerhagen. The colors were similar to Tiger 205.

Balthasar 'Bobby' Woll was a Tiger I commander in 1944. He received his Knight's Cross as Michael Wittmann's gunner. Woll poses shortly before going to Germany on sick leave.

American thrust designed to flank and surround Panzer Lehr and other Wehrmacht units. The 4th County of London Yeomanry (Sharpshooters), equipped with both Sherman and Cromwell tanks, led the British advance. The British objective was the road intersection at Villers-Bocage and the high country to the northeast – exactly the same as Michael Wittmann's objective for that fateful day. Watching the British advance from a point roughly south of Villers-Bocage, Wittmann was amazed to see elements of the British armored force – including Colonel Arthur Cranleigh's headquarters tank division – stop in the middle of Villers-Bocage to brew up some tea! Wittmann in his Tiger (Red 205) and his trusted gunner 'Bobby' Woll moved to the north through an orchard and successfully cut in behind the British A Company. Wittmann shot up everything in sight, resulting in a carnage straight out of Russia. These included the six headquarters Cromwell tanks, a further three M5A1 Honey light tanks, and approximately 25 additional armored fighting vehicles, including half tracks and Bren Gun Carriers. These were pure 'flock shoot' tactics – surprise and shock the enemy into disarray and pick him off almost at leisure. Wittmann was out of ammunition and low on fuel, forcing him to return to his observation post and switch to another fueled and armed tank, Tiger Red 222 of *SS-Untersharführer* Kurt Sowa. Wittmann led four LAH Tigers and one PzKpfw IV 'Special' from *Panzer Lehr* back through Villers-Bocage to the northeast to help other LAH Tigers that were attacking British A-Company tanks on the high ground. In the middle of Villers-Bocage, some British forces – including a squadron of tanks and some anti-tank guns – were hiding behind buildings. Three Tigers, Red 121, Red 112, and another Tiger of *SS-Hauptsturmführer* Mobius' 1st Company and the PzKpfw IV 'Special' were knocked out amid the swirling smoke. An up-gunned Sherman Firefly commanded by British Sergeant Bobby Bramall destroyed at least one vehicle. An anti-tank gun hit Wittmann's Tiger Red 222 in the left track. The crew abandoned the vehicle and escaped on foot towards the *Panzer Lehr* Division Headquarters some 3.7 miles (6 KM) north. The Germans later recovered Red 222 and used it again until it was destroyed in the fighting for the bridge at Stavelot. Wittmann returned with a company of PzKpfw IVs, which were reinforced by Mobius' remaining 1st Company Tigers. Villers-Bocage was captured and the remaining British tanks were destroyed and their crews were either killed or captured. The threat to *Panzer Lehr*'s flank was eliminated and the crossroads was still in German hands. Michael Wittmann had certainly inserted his personality on this battlefield and had forced the British to fight his way, which led them to defeat. Montgomery's thrust had been delayed for weeks because Wittmann had totally destroyed the spearhead of his elite armored division. Michael Wittmann was promoted to *SS-Hauptsturmführer* (Captain) for his action at Villers-Bocage and Adolf Hitler awarded the Swords to his Knight's Cross at Berchtesgaden on 22 June 1944. *Generalleutnant* (Lt. General) Fritz Bayerlein, *Panzer Lehr*'s commander, had nominated Wittmann for the Swords to his Knight's Cross for saving his division from encirclement. It was amazing for a member of the *Wehrmacht* (the regular German Army) to nominate a member of the *Waffen-SS* for an award. Wittmann's loyalty, bravery, and leadership transcended politics and petty in-fighting between military units.

***SS-Sturmbannführer* Jochen Peiper commanded the 1st Panzer Regiment, LAH Division. He presented Knight's Crosses to Michael Wittmann and 'Bobby' Woll on 14 January 1944.**

Wittmann ordered 'Bobby' Woll (now a Tiger commander) on medical leave on 2 August, due to recent injuries and combat fatigue. Woll initially refused to leave Wittmann and his comrades, but finally left, which probably saved his life. The Allies had launched six armored wedges to try to trap the retreating Germans in the infamous 'Falaise Pocket.' Wittmann and his crew in Tiger 'White 007' were killed near the village of St. Aignan-de-Cramesnil on 8 August 1944. Tiger 'White 007' was a *Stab* (Staff) Company command tank originally assigned to *SS-Standartenführe*r (Colonel) von Westerhagen. This command tank held some 30 fewer main gun rounds than a standard Tiger I, due to the space taken up by extra radio equipment for ground-to-air communications. During action, the 'turkey foot' antenna for the extra radio equipment was up and presented a target for Allied troops. Photos taken of Tiger 'White 007' show that the turret was blown off and landed upside-down some distance from the Tiger's hull. One version of Wittmann's death had him killed in a fierce fire-fight with Shermans of the British 33rd Armored Brigade. At least one Firefly (an up-gunned Sherman) hit Wittmann's Tiger, setting off the shells inside the tank. The other version had Wittmann's Tiger 'White 007' hit by rockets from a marauding Typhoon fighter-bomber. This author favors the last version, because he believes an experienced Tiger commander like Wittmann surely would not let himself be caught by enemy tanks, especially inferior Shermans. Many German tanks were trapped in the Falaise Pocket and destroyed by similar aerial attacks.

Panzer ace of aces Michael Wittmann's life ended in action in France. His final victory tally at the time he was awarded the Swords to the Knight's Cross was 138 enemy tanks destroyed and 132 anti-tanks guns blown up. He was a lower-class farm boy whose name became a household word in Germany. He fought during the invasion of Poland, during the Battle for France, in the Greek mountains, in the frozen Soviet winter, and in the killing-grounds of Normandy until there were no Tigers left. Wittmann was a brilliant tactician who could size up a battle and insert a single tank to destroy a whole armored unit and thereby change the entire battlefield to his liking. He could – and many times did – force a superior enemy to fight his way, which ended in tactical defeat for the enemy. An entire enemy tank division would cease to exist, as the shock of his unexpected attack shattered tanks as well as organization. Yet, he was a leader of men who would not accept his Knight's Cross until his enlisted gunner also received this medal. This treatment meant that his men would do anything for him.

German tank ace Michael Wittmann poses in Normandy on 22 June 1944. He soon received the Crossed Swords to his Knight's Cross for bravery and leadership at Villers-Bocage. Wittmann wears a leather Italian submarine jacket issued to elite panzer crews.

Oberstleutnant (Lt. Colonel) Walther Dahl

Walther Dahl was known as both the originator and destroyer of the *Sturmgruppe* concept of aerial warfare against Allied heavy bombers. The *Sturmgruppe* was first equipped with Messerschmitt Bf 109G-6s and later with Focke-Wulf Fw 190A-8 fighters, They were outfitted with extra armor and heavy weapons for the express purpose of attacking American B-17 and B-24 heavy bombers, which had proven most difficult for the German *Jagdwaffe* to bring down. Dahl was a top ace with 129 kills, including 30 heavy bombers.

Born on 27 March 1916, Dahl joined the *Wehrmacht* (German Army) in 1935. He was transferred to the Luftwaffe with the rank of *Leutnant* (2nd Lt.) in 1938. He successfully completed pilot training in 1939, after which he was assigned to *Jagdgeschwader* (JG; Fighter Wing) 3 during May of 1941. Dahl was late getting started, due to the time he spent in the army.

He scored his first victory over a Soviet fighter on 22 June 1941, the first day of Operation BARBAROSSA (the German invasion of the Soviet Union). Dahl had slowly racked up 17 kills by the end of October, but Dahl and 4./JG 3 was transferred to the Mediterranean theater on 13 December. During the next few months, he shot down a Spitfire Mk V over Malta. On 10 April 1942, he was transferred for a time to the JG 3 reserve squadron and was away from the front while engaged in training duties. Dahl was then attached to the Headquarters Group (*Stab*) JG 3 on 15 August. This *Stab* was heavily involved in the fighting in Russia. He scored on a regular basis and knocked down his 50th Soviet aircraft on 16 April 1943. On 30 July, he was promoted to *Hauptmann* (Captain) and assigned to command III./JG 3.

JG 3 was redeployed West to defend the Homeland from waves of Allied bombers. Bomber interception was a highly different type of combat than the German fighter pilots were used to in Russia. Aerial combat over the steppes was usually tactical in nature and fought at low level. In the West, groups of fighters maneuvered against one another at high altitude while heavy bombers flew in trying to destroy German cities. Walther Dahl shot down his first heavy bomber on 6 September 1944. By 11 March, his total had reached 67 kills and for this he was awarded the Knight's Cross and was promoted to Major. Dahl's techniques for attacking heavy bombers were especially highly regarded by this time. His *sturm* (storm) tactics centered on slow cavalry-type charges with specially armed and armored fighters arranged line abreast moving up from the rear on bombers boxes of four-engine bombers. This line of fighters would fire only when they were at point blank range. They had to withstand .50 caliber (12.7MM) return fire from rearward-pointing machine guns during their slow charge into firing position. Once they fired in concert, several heavy bombers would be knocked out of the sky and almost always the German pilots would take heavy casualties. This was no place for the faint of heart.

Walther Dahl devised *sturm* tactics against heavy bombers and led his men by example. He continued to fly operational missions until the end of World War Two.

Dahl was able to put his ideas into action when he was placed in command of a heavy bomber special attack group on 21 May. Because of Dahl's success, the test group was restructured as IV.(*Sturm*)/JG 3 and II.(*Sturm*)/JG 300. Walther Dahl was placed in command of JG 3 and then was made Kommodore of JG 300 on 7 July. His personal score stood at 75 kills by September of 1944.

On 26 January 1945, Dahl was placed in charge of daylight fighters. Following the removal of *Generalleutnant* Adolf Galland (103 kills), *Oberst* (Colonel) Gordon Gollob (150 kills) had taken over his position on orders from Hermann Göring (22 kills in World War One) and the loyal Dahl answered directly to Gollob. Galland went on to command *Jagdverband* (JV; Fighter Formation) 44, an Me 262 jet fighter unit. A promotion like this ordinarily meant the end of active duty as a fighter pilot; however, Dahl continued to lead by example and fly combat missions. His score reached 92 kills on 1 February 1945, when he was awarded the Oak Leaves to the Knight's Cross. He tallied 100 victories on 28 February.

Dahl switched to the innovative Me 262A-1a in March of 1945. He scored another 29 victories by the end of World War Two, including two P-47 Thunderbolts on 27 March and a P-51D Mustang on 26 April. Not all these last kills were scored with the Me 262. Dahl's best scoring occurred late in the war under horrible conditions when Germany was collapsing. He did not have to fly combat missions at this time, but he continued to do so. He flew 678 combat missions and 45 of his 129 victories came in against Allied bombers. His total of 30 heavy bombers shot down is the third best in history. Dahl also scored several kills while flying jet fighters. He passed away in Heidelberg at the age of 69 on 25 November 1985.

Major Clarence E. 'Bud' Anderson, Jr.

Clarence E. 'Bud' Anderson, Jr. was born in Oakland, California on 12 January 1922. He attended Sacramento Junior College and joined the US Army Air Forces (USAAF) on 19 January 1942. He graduated from the Aviation Cadet program on 29 September 1942 – Anderson was a late starter in World War Two.

Anderson was assigned to the 363rd Fighter Squadron (FS), 357th Fighter Group (FG) to get more training at Tonopah, Nevada with the lackluster Bell P-39 Airacobra. Following this, he and the 357th FG was sent to England in November of 1943. They were supplied with the new North American P-51 Mustang fighter, which was powered by the British-designed Merlin engine. This addition turned the mediocre Mustang into an excellent long-range interceptor that could range out ahead of the bombers to disrupt enemy aerial activity. The long-range Mustang was responsible for the demise of the Jagdwaffe heavy fighter activity against US daylight bomber streams. The Messerschmitt Bf 110G and Me 210 twin-engine fighters were no match for the high performance Mustangs and were swept from the Reich skies.

'Bud' Anderson, now a captain, entered combat with his unit over Dessau, Germany on 20 February 1943. He damaged, but did not knock down a Bf 109G. He had to wait until 8 March before scoring his first victory, another Bf 109G, near Hannover. On 11 April, he shot down a Bf 109G, damaged another, and shared in a kill over a twin-engine He 111K medium bomber. Anderson scored two victories over Fw 190A fighters during late April and early May to become an ace on 8 May. Anderson was sent on a rest tour to the United States, something his German counterparts were never allowed.

Anderson returned to combat with his old unit, the 363rd FS. He immediately shot down two Fw 190A fighters and was credited with a third probable during an intense, drawn out fight on 27 November 1944. His last victories came on 5 December 1944, when he downed two confirmed Fw 190As and another probable. He ended the war with 16.25 confirmed victories along with two probables and two damaged.

Anderson had good vision and situational awareness, which enabled him to line up several enemy fighters for a series of 'bounces' (attacks from above) that led to multiple kills. His friend Chuck Yeager (11.5 kills) said Anderson had lightning reactions, which coupled with the high performance Mustang to make him a formidable fighter pilot. Had

'Bud' Anderson sits on the wing of his P-51 Mustang, OLD CROW.

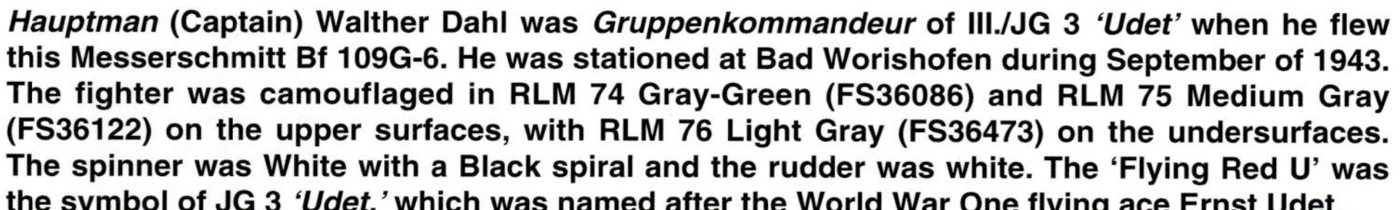

Hauptman (Captain) Walther Dahl was *Gruppenkommandeur* of III./JG 3 *'Udet'* when he flew this Messerschmitt Bf 109G-6. He was stationed at Bad Worishofen during September of 1943. The fighter was camouflaged in RLM 74 Gray-Green (FS36086) and RLM 75 Medium Gray (FS36122) on the upper surfaces, with RLM 76 Light Gray (FS36473) on the undersurfaces. The spinner was White with a Black spiral and the rudder was white. The 'Flying Red U' was the symbol of JG 3 *'Udet,'* which was named after the World War One flying ace Ernst Udet.

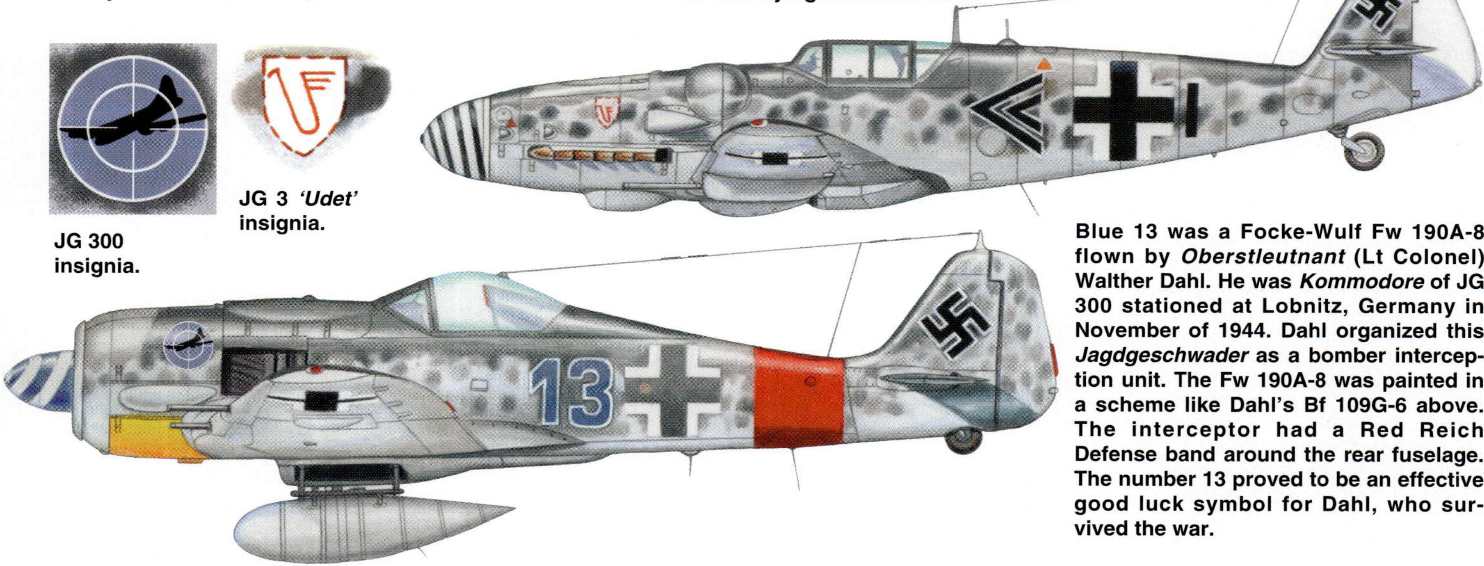

JG 300 insignia.

JG 3 *'Udet'* insignia.

Blue 13 was a Focke-Wulf Fw 190A-8 flown by *Oberstleutnant* (Lt Colonel) Walther Dahl. He was *Kommodore* of JG 300 stationed at Lobnitz, Germany in November of 1944. Dahl organized this *Jagdgeschwader* as a bomber interception unit. The Fw 190A-8 was painted in a scheme like Dahl's Bf 109G-6 above. The interceptor had a Red Reich Defense band around the rear fuselage. The number 13 proved to be an effective good luck symbol for Dahl, who survived the war.

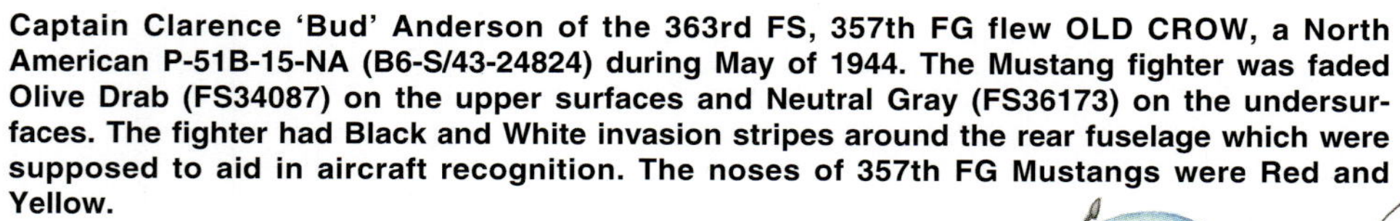

Captain Clarence 'Bud' Anderson of the 363rd FS, 357th FG flew OLD CROW, a North American P-51B-15-NA (B6-S/43-24824) during May of 1944. The Mustang fighter was faded Olive Drab (FS34087) on the upper surfaces and Neutral Gray (FS36173) on the undersurfaces. The fighter had Black and White invasion stripes around the rear fuselage which were supposed to aid in aircraft recognition. The noses of 357th FG Mustangs were Red and Yellow.

Captain 'Bud' Anderson flew this brand new P-51D-10-NA Mustang (B6-S/44-14450) during late 1944. It was finished in British paint similar to Olive Drab, but with more green (close to FS34094) on the upper surfaces and Neutral Gray on the under surfaces. This fighter had invasion stripes only on the undersurfaces below the national insignia. This style of long range drop tank was made of paper maché and glue, which lasted just long enough to get the US fighters over central Germany, where they were dropped.

This is the same Mustang (B6-S/44-14450) as above, but with the Olive and Neutral Gray paint removed to expose the natural metal. The fighter ended up with a Red tail and Red and Yellow nose. Olive Drab was retained in front of the cockpit as an anti-glare panel, with the name OLD CROW in White. Anderson ended the war with 16.25 kills, which were indicated by kill marks under the cockpit.

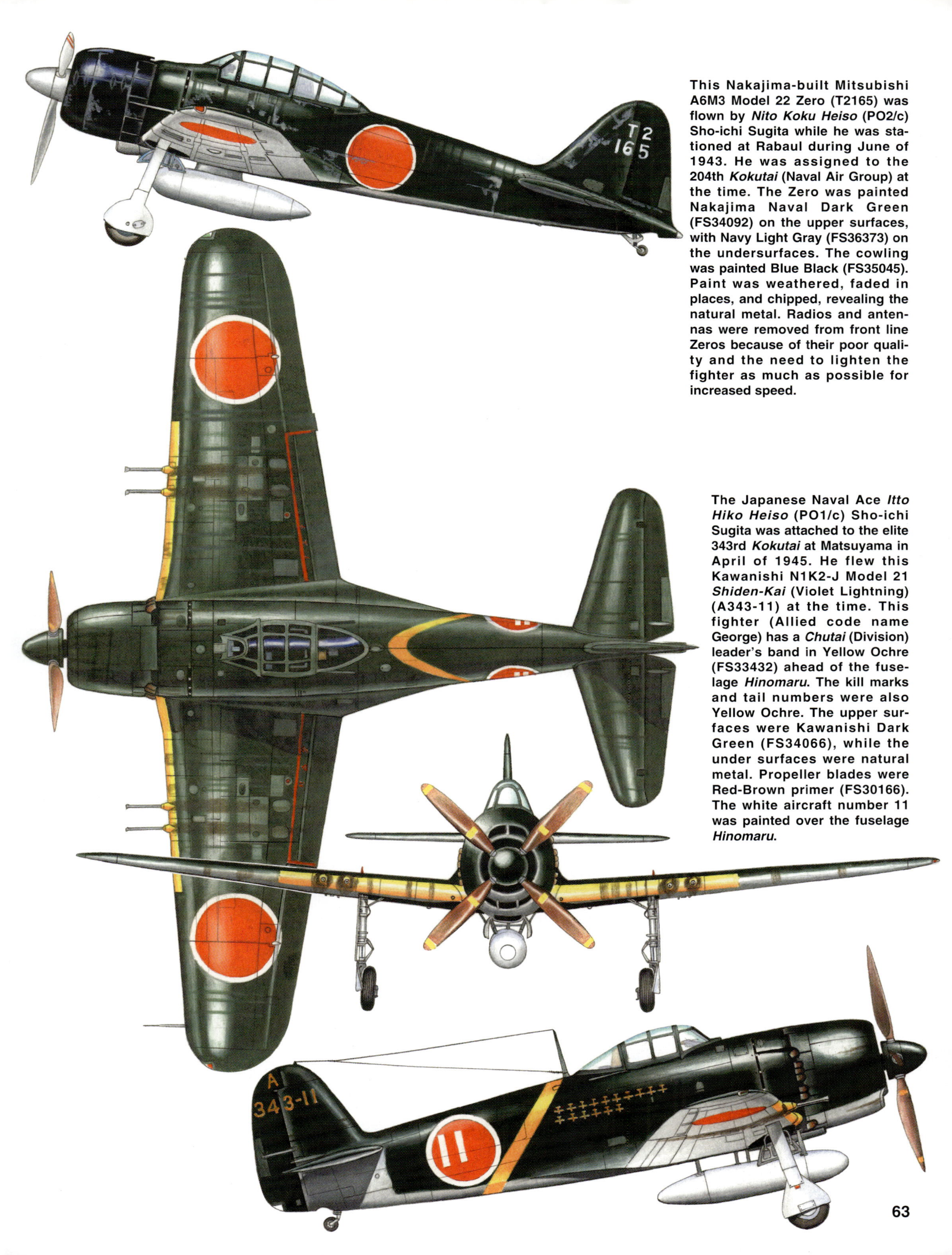

This Nakajima-built Mitsubishi A6M3 Model 22 Zero (T2165) was flown by *Nito Koku Heiso* (PO2/c) Sho-ichi Sugita while he was stationed at Rabaul during June of 1943. He was assigned to the 204th *Kokutai* (Naval Air Group) at the time. The Zero was painted Nakajima Naval Dark Green (FS34092) on the upper surfaces, with Navy Light Gray (FS36373) on the undersurfaces. The cowling was painted Blue Black (FS35045). Paint was weathered, faded in places, and chipped, revealing the natural metal. Radios and antennas were removed from front line Zeros because of their poor quality and the need to lighten the fighter as much as possible for increased speed.

The Japanese Naval Ace *Itto Hiko Heiso* (PO1/c) Sho-ichi Sugita was attached to the elite 343rd *Kokutai* at Matsuyama in April of 1945. He flew this Kawanishi N1K2-J Model 21 *Shiden-Kai* (Violet Lightning) (A343-11) at the time. This fighter (Allied code name George) has a *Chutai* (Division) leader's band in Yellow Ochre (FS33432) ahead of the fuselage *Hinomaru*. The kill marks and tail numbers were also Yellow Ochre. The upper surfaces were Kawanishi Dark Green (FS34066), while the under surfaces were natural metal. Propeller blades were Red-Brown primer (FS30166). The white aircraft number 11 was painted over the fuselage *Hinomaru*.

Anderson been in combat longer, he would have racked up many more victories. He remained in the US Air Force following World War Two and commanded an F-86 squadron during the Korean War, but scored no kills during this conflict. He went on to command the 355th Tactical Fighter Wing (TFW) flying F-105 Thunderchief fighter-bombers during the Vietnam War. Following retirement from the Air Force on 1 March 1972, Anderson worked for McDonnell Douglas Aircraft Corporation and directed their flight test facility at Edwards AFB, California.

Sho-i (Ensign) Sho-ichi Sugita

Sho-ichi Sugita, who was to become one of Japan's highest scoring aces, was born in Niigata Prefecture in 1924. The aircraft bug bit the young Sugita, like so many other young men of his age. He dropped out of agriculture school at age 15 in 1940 to join the Imperial Japanese Navy (IJN). Sugita graduated from flight training in March of 1942 and – after serving in the Battle of Midway that June – was assigned to the 204th *Kokutai* (Naval Air Group) at Buin, Bougainville Island in October.

Sugita fought his first combats against extremely hard to shoot down USAAF heavy bombers. On 1 December 1942, he shared in the downing of a B-17 Flying Fortress over his airfield at Buin. Sugita closed to ramming distance and fired at point blank range into the large bomber. The wing of his A6M Zero struck the B-17 during this engagement, but he returned safely to his base. Sugita shared in the destruction of another B-17 on 28 December and fought a swirling dogfight with F4F Wildcats of Marine Fighter Squadron One Twenty One (VMF-121) over Munda Point, New Georgia on 2 January 1943. He claimed one of the stubby Grummans out of two destroyed on this date. By month's end, Sugita had shot down three more F4F fighters and shared in the downing of another B-24 Liberator. He was beginning to master his A6M3 Zero.

Sugita had seven victories to his credit when he and five other Zero pilots were selected to escort two G4M1 (Betty) bombers on 18 April 1943. The G4M1s were transporting *Taisho* (Admiral) Isoroku Yamamoto – Commander-in-Chief of the Combined Fleet – and his staff. Intelligence code-breaking alerted US forces in the region and long-range USAAF P-38 Lightnings from Guadalcanal intercepted and shot down both bombers over Bougainville. Sugita claimed two of the P-38s in the wild dogfight that followed. He probably shot down First Lieutenant Raymond Hine, who was lost during the fight. The returning Japanese fighter pilots shared collective blame for the loss of the popular *Taisho* Yamamoto and they were given every chance to redeem their honor by death in combat. The six fighter pilots threw caution to the wind as they engaged American attackers with increasingly obsolescent Zero fighters. Four of these six pilots were soon dead and Kenji Yanagiya (eight kills), the fifth, was sent back to Japan with severe wounds. Sugita was different in that the increasing levels of dangerous combat allowed him to hone his skills and he became the deadliest of foes. He seemed to thrive and gain in stature and ability with each combat. Fellow pilots revered Sugita, especially the younger ones that completed flight training since the beginning of World War Two.

Sugita flew an A6M3 Model 22 Zero when he shot down two VMF-112 F4U Corsairs over Guadalcanal on 12 June 1943. Several days later, he shot down another VMF-112 Corsair and his final F4U kill came on 25 August. His favorite tactic against these large and fast fighters was to fight them in the vertical plane, where his Zero held a climb advantage. Sugita was shot down by VMF-214 Corsair pilots over the Shortlands on 26 August 1943. He was forced to bail out of his stricken fighter with severe burns. He was rescued from the sea and sent back to Japan for recovery. It is interesting to note that the younger group of Japanese Naval Air Force (JNAF) fighter pilots wore parachutes, unlike earlier pilots like Saburo Sakai (64).

Sugita was then assigned to the 263rd *Kokutai* and fought in violent air battles over the Caroline and Mariana Islands. He was part of a six Zero flight that was intercepted near Yap Island by VF-31 Hellcats. Five of the six Zeros were shot down, while Sugita made an emergency landing on Peleliu Island. The flight leader, *Tai-i* (Lieutenant) Yasuhiro Shigematsu (ten kills), died in this action. Some time later, Sugita and the remaining 263rd *Kokutai* pilots escaped north to the Philippines, where they were assigned to the 201st *Kokutai*. Once again, Sugita found himself in the middle of bone-crushing combat and once again he thrived on a steady diet of flaming aircraft, red-hot tracers, and increasingly superior US fighters. It was once rumored that he shot down Captain Thomas McGuire (38) – the second-highest scoring US P-38 ace – and his wingman. This version of McGuire's death has been superceded by another version, in which determined Japanese Army Air Force (JAAF) pilots downed the great American ace. Sugita was transferred from the Philippines in January of 1945, after he had outlasted most of his fellow 201st *Kokutai* fighter pilots.

Taisa (Captain) Minoru Genda, who did not believe in the *Kamakaze* (Divine Wind) suicide philosophy, formed an elite fighter *Kokutai* at Matsuyama in December of 1944. This new 343rd *Kokutai* was equipped with the equally new N1K2-J *Shiden-Kai* (Violet Lightning) interceptor fighter. The Allies assigned the code name George to this new fighter, which had a similar performance envelope to the Corsair. Genda personally selected Sugita to lead a *Shotai* (Flight) of four aircraft and later to head a *Chutai* (Division) of eight aircraft with the new *Hikotai* (Squadron) 301 (16 aircraft). Early in World War Two, a *Shotai* consisted of three aircraft and a *Chutai* was made up of three *Shotai* or nine aircraft. Late in the war, the JNAF had copied US formations made up of two fighters followed loosely by another two. This was originally the *rotte* developed by the Germans during combat in the Spanish Civil War.

Sugita's *Shotai* shot down three USN Hellcats during their first combat over Kure, Japan on 19 March 1945. On 15 April, Sugita and his wingman *Nito Koku Heiso* (PO2/c) Toyomi Miyazawa were shot down and killed by Hellcat pilot Lt Cdr Robert 'Doc' Weatherup of VF-46. Sugita tried to take off with his wingman as Weatherup and his Hellcats launched rockets and strafed Kanoya Field. Sugita never had a chance as Weatherup had superior speed and altitude while he slid in behind Sugita's *Shiden-Kai* and poured machine gun fire into the Japanese fighter. Sho-ichi Sugita, hero of Japan, died in a ball of fire as his kill-marked *Shiden-Kai* smashed into the ground at the end of the airfield. Miyazawa was shot down moments later.

Taisa Genda gave a posthumous citation to Sho-ichi Sugita on 1 August 1945. Sugita was recognized for scoring 70 individual kills and 40 shared victories, which was an amazing score for a late-war Japanese fighter pilot. He was promoted two ranks to that of *Sho-i* (Ensign) at the time of his death.

Sho-ichi Sugita was known as a reckless fighter pilot, which was probably left over from the failed Yamamoto escort mission. He was able to temper this wild side by a massive amount of experience gained from volunteering for the most dangerous missions. He always turned without hesitation into attacks with both the Zero and the *Shiden-Kai*. He was able to successfully engage both Hellcats and Corsairs with the inferior A6M3 Model 22 Zero by fighting them in the vertical plane. The Zero had a better climb rate than either of the heavier US fighters. Sugita would follow Hellcats and Corsairs up to altitude after their diving and climbing attacks, many times shooting them down when they least expected to be attacked. The *Shiden-Kai* was a late-war Zero replacement and was superior to the Hellcat in most respects. Its performance was similar in speed and climb to later F4U Corsair variants, but had better maneuverability due to hydraulic combat flaps. The *Shiden-Kai* could make around 405 MPH (652 KMH) with high quality aviation gasoline and lubricants. The lesser quality gasoline available to the late war IJN meant that the *Shiden-Kai* could make only approximately 370 MPH (595 KMH), or approximately the same speed as a Hellcat. Sho-ichi Sugita was a deadly adversary and perhaps one of the best enemy fighter pilots ever to clash with the US Navy and Army Air Forces.

Sho-ichi Sugita was one of the Zero escort pilots for Admiral Isoroku Yamamoto's G4M1 bomber when P-38s intercepted them. The admiral's bomber was one of two shot down that day.